What writers

"An exacting and lively writer."

— Steve Martin
comedian and author of *Born Standing Up*
and *Pure Drivel*

"Starshine's columns are so witty, wise and observant that I wish I wrote them. Her voice is hip and contemporary but it's also humane and sensible. She's Erma Bombeck for the 21st century."

— Jane Heller
author of *Some Nerve* and *An Ex to Grind*

"A wonderful writer, with a sense of humor and strong point of view."

— J.J. Abrams
writer/creator of *Lost* and *Cloverfield*

"She's a fresh and flat-out funny writer with a special talent for seeing and showing the absurd and the joyful in the ordinary and the everyday."

— Jerry Roberts
former managing editor, *San Francisco Chronicle*, and author of *Dianne Feinstein: Never Let Them See You Cry*

"Starshine has an irresistible voice with a pitch-perfect ear for the hilarity, anxiety and quiet desperation of parenthood."

— Ann Louise Bardach
Vanity Fair contributor and
author of *Cuba Confidential*

"Ms. Roshell's work has a seemingly effortless glow. She's one of our generation's most winning columnists."

— Jeff Gordinier
editor, *Details* magazine, and
author of *X Saves the World*

"When words fail us, Starshine is there to speak for the girl in all of us women. She articulates thoughts we didn't even know we had."

— Cheri Steinkellner
Emmy-winning writer, *Cheers*

"She writes about the joys and travails of parenting with grace and understanding. This father and grandfather finds her columns useful and insightful — and she always makes me laugh."

— Lou Cannon
author of *Ronald Reagan: A Life in Politics*
and *Official Negligence*

★ Keep Your Skirt On ★

CABAL © PUBLISHING
SANTA BARBARA, CA

KICKY COLUMNS WITH LEGS
by
Starshine Roshell

Copyright © 2008 Starshine Roshell.

All rights reserved.

Published in the United States by Cabal Publishing
www.KeepYourSkirtOn.com

ISBN 978-0-9766761-4-0

First edition

Cover illustration by Tim Sale
Photograph by Jacky Sallow
Design and layout by John Roshell

Visit Starshine on the web at
www.StarshineRoshell.com

DEDICATED TO JG,
WHO TOLD ME, "YOU
REALLY SHOULD EXPLAIN
HOW WOMEN THINK.
BECAUSE WE GUYS —
WE DON'T KNOW
THESE THINGS."

★ Contents ★

Acknowledgments 11

'BROAD' APPEAL

Pole Positions 17
She's Great. Him I Hate. 20
Nipping Sniggers in the Bud 23
Floss This 26
Sex Drive? 29
Mop Scene 32
Fertile Fashion 35
Doppeldressers 38
Go With the Flow 41
A Gal in the Guys' Gym 44
Designer Vaginas 47
Love Bites 50
Everything I Know About Men
   I Learned at Strip Clubs 53
A Week of Strong 56
Watch Her Strut 59

NEWS TO ME

Talula Does the Hula From Hawaii 65
Obama, Sweetie 68
X Appeal 71
Palin Comparison 74
The Great Disney Smoke-Out 77
Turning the Other Cheek on Spanking 80
I Now Pronounce You Sissy and Wife 83
Cold-Hearted or Hot-Blooded? 86
Innocence Glossed 90
Going Gay 93
Warning: Children in Charge 96
Shaking My Faith in Quad 99
Sinning Senators Are So Ho-Hum 102
Here's the Buzz 105
Church and State Collide on Highway 108
Mommy's a Liar 111
A Formula for Guilt 114
Another Sticky Mess for O.J. 117

ONLY KIDDING

The Swing of Things 123
I Killed the Tooth Fairy 126
Mom Envy 129
Hang the Potty 132
Thank You, Officer. No, Really. 135
You Camp Be Serious 138

Once Upon a Cool Mom 141
Old Wives vs. New Science 144
Swearing Off New Year's Promises 147
Mothering the Mothers 150
Do You Have to Like Your Kids? 153
Party Favor 156
Growing by Bleeps and Bounds..................... 159
The Third-Grader's Guide to Girls 162
Spring Cleaning 165
The Game of LIFE 168
Phantom Tiara Syndrome 171
Who Wants to Be a Cotillionaire? 174

CULTURE PEARLS

Flights of Fancy 179
My First Fisticuffs 182
Numb and Number... 185
Cyber Sleuthing 188
Smellywood's Puttin' on the Spritz 191
Down With Uptalk 194
Email Embarrassment..................................... 197
My New Stud... 200
I'm Virtually Popular! 203
A Croc of Shoe 206
Facebook Friendships Hard to Ignore........... 209
The Slutty Mechanic....................................... 212
Thank You For Coming, Now Get Out 215

FAMILY, CANDIDLY

Mancations 221
Road Trip, a.k.a Chaos in a Box 224
Powerless Steering 227
The Nana-Fest Manifesto 230
Where Are the Homeless
    When You Need 'Em? 233
Ode to Real Love 236
My Father's Gift 239
The Stuff Slough 242
Merry Solstice 245
Me Time 248

WRITE OR WRONG

Diary of a Protest Virgin 253
If I Ran the Zoo 256
Taking the Stand 259
How to Love Hate Mail 262

★ Acknowledgments ★

SOME PEOPLE CHOOSE friends based on how nice they are. Not me. I'm not inspired by nice. I surround myself with people who are smarter, funnier and braver than me — and then I drag them into my columns.

My silent partners are the trusty Chicks of the Round Table, a cadre of clever gal pals who respond quickly and candidly to my requests for intimate insight into spanking, lying and Googling ex-boyfriends. They give great quote.

My husband John hears from his basketball buddies when I embarrass him in print, but he doesn't hear this often enough from me: You are an authentic prince. And an exceedingly forgiving one at that.

A thousand thanks to the Read Naked Book Club for its column-fueling girl talk; to ingenious *Parent Trip* author Jenna McCarthy for all my best kickers (my mantra: What Would Jenna Do?); to Andrea Huebner, the Voice of Riesling, the best editor I ever had, who shows me by example that anything worth doing is worth doing perfectly; to Carole Ingraham, who makes me laugh like no one else can by ever upping the "inappropriate" ante; and to the lovely Rori Trovato for modeling the freelance-is-freedom philosophy with unparalleled panache.

I hail the virtues of my courageous former *News-Press* colleagues who risked their livelihoods — and the readers who cancelled their subscriptions — in the name of quality journalism; and Jerry Roberts, who embodies the curiosity and integrity of our trade; the wise Tom Jacobs, for sending me kooky news; my dear friend and talented illustrator Al Bonowitz; Michael Seabaugh, the only columnist in the world who's as charming in person as in print; my earliest mentors, Allen Parsons and Melinda Johnson; and Gary Robb, for reminding me to put on my big-girl panties and deal.

I adore the *Santa Barbara Independent* for welcoming me and making me ever-so-much-cooler by association, the can-do Kate Schwab for nudging me out of my comfort zone, and Frank Goss for treating me like an artist even though I write about flossing.

Deepest gratitude to my mother Tera, grandmother Vicki and grandmother Bette — who speak their minds and fear no one. And my father Doug, whose love of language and affinity for the absurd spills onto my pages. And Stu, who made me rewrite my fifth grade essays until they were (finally) good.

Thank you, Dennis and Nancy Gaushell, for the haven where I write.

And to my boys, Stone and Dash, for their fresh perspectives, ebullient characters and for reminding me daily what matters.

Pole Positions

IT STARTED OUT as an innocent evening, with plans to meet a girlfriend for a local book-signing.

But when it was over, there were feathers on my chest, lube in my hair and a new place in my heart for stripper poles.

My friend and I had gone to meet Miyoko Fujimori, author of "The Housewife's Guide to the Practical Striptease," who was hawking her how-to at the local lingerie shop. Purrmission is a sweet little boutique that peddles elegant underthings at the front of the store, and blush-inducing boudoir toys in the back.

Owner Melanie Doctors, who goes by the name Miss Kitty, was trussed up for the evening in a leather bustier and black feather miniskirt.

"I don't usually dress like Big Bird," she explained, but tonight was special. Miyoko, an exotic dancer-cum-mother of two, was not only going to autograph her purse-sized disrobing manual; she was going to teach us some man-pleasing moves on a portable stripper pole.

Raunchy debauchery or constructive instruction?

"It's every woman's right to explore her sexuality," insisted Miss Kitty, and unless you live on ABC's Wisteria Lane, housewives are especially desperate for a way to bust up the monotony of monogamy.

If marriage saps our sexual energy, motherhood darn near drains it dry. Maybe it's all the other physical demands — breastfeeding, extricating a flailing toddler from a grocery cart, eternally plucking toys and socks and straw wrappers from the living room floor.

That stuff just sucks the swing from your step, you know what I mean?

That's where Miyoko and her stripping primer slink in.

A former Miss Teen Seattle and host of several Playboy TV shows, Miyoko, 32, knows it's hard to "turn it on" after an evening of sorting laundry and reading bedtime stories. But she swears stripping can put us back in touch with our sensual selves, and help us shed the psychological confines that our daily uniforms impose.

"Once our clothes hit the floor, we are free to be anyone we want to be," which, for Miyoko, could be a shy schoolgirl, a friendly cowgirl or — come on, no judgment here — a firefighter.

"Step, bend and turn out," she explained while guiding 20 or so women slowly, individually around the silver pole. Several were moms from a local elementary school. With Prince on the stereo and feather boas around our necks, we learned a sultry headroll and a seductive hip lift.

It was exhilaratingly fun — which explains why so many celebrities are doing it. No surprise that Pam Anderson and Paris Hilton have permanent poles in their homes, or that a shnockered Lindsay Lohan and Kate Moss got friendly with a pole at a New York strip club earlier this year. But the trend has gone mainstream: Kate Hudson had one installed at her house. "Desperate Housewife" Teri Hatcher demonstrated her stripper moves on Leno. And just this month, proper Brit Emma Thompson busted out some impromptu pole love on "Ellen."

Miyoko's book offers practical tips on what to wear, how to move and where to, um, shave before a domestic performance. She also advises readers not to dwell on our bodies' imperfections, but to direct our dude's attention to exactly what we want him to see: "The slope of your neck, the bounce in your breasts, the sparkle in your eyes."

I like that. I also like the two reasons she says a matrimonial striptease is better than one in a nudie bar: A wife knows exactly what her husband likes — she's not guessing.

And his odds of scoring are 100 percent better.

She's Great. Him I Hate.

THERE'S YOUR BEST FRIEND. Smart. Funny. Laidback. Almost never smells bad. Then there's your best friend's spouse. Ignorant. Juvenile. Fat head lodged firmly up fanny.

We all have someone we cherish — who cherishes someone we hate. The awkward dynamic utterly upends the joy of socializing, leaving us languishing between two crappy choices:

1. See less of your beloved buddy.

2. Submit to social occasions during which you pretend to enjoy yourself but are in fact quietly horrified by the mean, moronic, or nacho cheese-flavored things spewing out of your buddy's sweetheart's stupid face.

It's a fairly common problem, according to my friends, who I hope to god are not referring to me or my husband when they disclose the following stories.

"Usually, if my pal is cool, his or her partner is cool, too," said an amiga of mine. But ... "One of our longtime buddies married an idiot. She's dumb and opinionated — a really bad combo. Loud, tacky, just plain scary. We never see him anymore."

Avoidance is one solution. Confrontation is another. A gal I know opted for outright honesty when her free-spirited friend began dating a surly and controlling ass. "I told her she deserves to be happier, but that I love her no matter what," she said. The disappointing result: "She's pissed I don't like her guy. It's definitely cooled our friendship."

If the relationship is a marriage, and not just a fling, the truth gets trickier. "In my experience, it's best not to tell someone they married a loser," said a guy whose sister — sadly — did just that. "He's a blowhard know-nothing and a self-centered jerk whose favorite response in an argument is, 'Duh!'" He tolerates the fellow by finding common ground. "When I have to be with him, I try to keep things focused on sports. It seems safer."

Divide-and-conquer is another popular tactic. A woman I know had a friend whose husband spit food when he talked, asked way too many personal questions, and had really long fingernails with dirt under them. "He wasn't a serial killer. He just made me gag," she said. "I didn't want to lose this friend, so I always suggested she and I have lunch, just the two of us. But she would always drag him along. Eventually, we drifted apart."

Plotting twosomes and drafting tepid talking points may actually be the easiest part of the calamitous-couple conundrum. Harder is having to reevaluate your friend based on his or her shockingly bad taste in bedfellows.

"My best friend of 14 years was very funny and one of the most intelligent humans I've had the pleasure of hanging out with," said a lady I know. "Her boyfriend would greet me with a bear hug and a big juicy kiss, leaving me smelling like his aftershave. I felt like a fire hydrant that had been pissed upon. He was small-minded and mean-spirited in private, but a good ol' boy in public. Yuck."

She learned to avoid the hugs — but she could never embrace her friend's choice. "After she married him, my admiration for her began to erode quickly," she said. "As time goes by, aging, money, family, responsibilities, and shifting priorities change our character for good or ill. Sometimes it brings us together, sometimes it moves us apart."

It's okay to not love a chum's lover, but it's best to keep this in mind: You're not the only person equipped with the gag reflex. "I was on the other end of this scenario once," said my girlfriend. "I had super-close, longtime friends who loathed my first husband. As it turned out, I ended up loathing him, too."

'BROAD' APPEAL

Nipping Sniggers in the Bud

THE WAY SHE WAS mocked, chastised, and condemned for the evening's biggest fashion "oops," you'd think Ellen Pompeo had arrived at the Golden Globes in a gown of gleaming panda bear pelts. But what was the *Grey's Anatomy* actress's actual crime?

She dared to show up on the red carpet — on a chilly January night — with her nipples visibly standing at attention beneath her white Versace dress.

"It's white," smirked E! Channel host Ryan Seacrest when the actress paused for an on-camera interview. "And ... it's cold."

I need to explain something that men don't seem to understand: This is not a female erection.

Unless Pompeo was wild with lust for Seacrest — hello, have you seen her fiancé? — the phenomenon taking place at the end of her breasts was simply a full-frontal form of goose bumps. The result of temperature, and nothing more. So why should it inspire sniggering?

"Three words," explained a frank and bodacious girlfriend of mine. "Boys are dumb."

Men like to dream up — or even drum up — eroticism where there is absolutely none, she said. "I dated a guy in college who worked at a grocery store. I used to stop by to see him and he would always find a reason to shuttle me to the frozen food section."

Male friends of mine insist they understand the basic physiology — that nipples' abundant nerve endings cause the surrounding muscle to contract in response to cold, friction, sexual excitement, and even nervousness. And that when it happens in public, it's almost never because the woman's looking for action. But they don't care. They think it's hot.

"Please!" said one. "I'm not going to let reality interfere with my little nipple-inspired fantasies."

Two things happen, though, when women are treated as sex objects simply for forgetting to wear a sweater — and I should point out the double standard that no one calls Simon Cowell a slut, though his nipples are as prominent a part of *American Idol* as Paula Abdul's dilated pupils. First, we begin to feel self-conscious about something as involuntary as a sneeze. And products like Nippits Nipple Covers, which promise to conceal any sign of chill "even under wet swimsuits," don't exactly counteract the shame.

"I think everyone has a different sensitivity level on the subject, which has as much to do with your age as the situation in which it happens, bar-hopping versus boardroom meeting, and how much decolletage you are working with," said a friend of mine. A busty gal, she was once horrified to see "an adolescent boy alerting all his friends to my — ahem — condition."

The other casualty of this way of thinking is that women begin to turn on one another — and no, fellas, I don't mean we turn each other on. I mean we judge and snipe at other women for failing to get their areolas under controlla.

"It's always a little inappropriate," confirmed another girlfriend. "I had an employee whose nipples were always showing and usually at odd angles, and I always thought she should do something about it. It made everyone uncomfortable."

Times may be slowly changing. On television, the mere glimpse of a protruding nipple used to send Standards and Practices watchdogs scurrying for their "CENSORED" stamps. Now Jennifer Aniston is allowed to flit about the *Friends* set with her breasts set on permanent frost alert. And we can all titter as Samantha struts through *Sex and the City* wearing silicone falsies that maintain an eye-catching boi-oi-oing under her blouse at all times.

If any real good is to come from snide comments about Ellen Pompeo's golden globes, women must wear our bosom buttons with pride. "Science" and "sexy" can exist side by side, under the same shirt, can't they?

"I was pretty ambivalent about the whole nipple thing, until I nursed two kids," said my buddy, she of-frozen-food-aisle fame. "Now, when the pointer sisters stand at attention, they pull all that loose, sagging skin with them and — for a few magical moments — I actually have a decent looking rack again. Who can find fault with that?"

Floss This

I'M GOING TO TELL YOU a secret, but you have to promise it won't leave this page. Because it's kind of gross, and sure to damage my standing among the more hygienic members of society: I don't floss. I just don't. And I'm tired of apologizing for it.

Every six months my dental hygienist — a very sweet woman when she is not wielding pointy tools and preaching bacterial fire and brimstone — reminds me that my slacker approach to oral health is a dangerous game. She threatens me with gum disease and implies that when I fail to root out the evil lurking between my bicuspids, the terrorists have won.

I look appropriately ashamed and vow to dust off the box of mint-flavored string in my medicine cabinet and hunt down the plaque-breeding bastards with everything I've got. But we both know I won't do it. Because — and here's where dentists may get cranky — I have a life.

It's not a glamorous life, or even an especially

interesting one. But like those of most working moms, it's busy. It's full of grocery shopping and laundry folding, homework checking and carpool driving, deadline meeting and invoice tracking. There are birthday cards to be mailed, flu shots to be scheduled, and property taxes to be scrounged up.

I realize that my incisors are untidy, and I accept it with the same exasperated shrug I give to my limp houseplants, unwashed dog, and hard water-stained stemware. The floor of my car is littered with empty water bottles, the wall of my dining room bears a grimy handprint that — no kidding — has been there for two years, and there's a junk drawer in my bathroom I don't even want to tell you about. But I'm supposed to fixate on a little tartar?

If I set aside the three nightly minutes it would take to floss my teeth and applied it instead to, say, reading a page of a classic novel, I could have finished *The Sun Also Rises* this year. I could have done 27,450 sit-ups or purged 5,795 emails from my inbox. My Christmas cards would already be addressed, stamped, and stuffed.

The point is there are so many things we should all be doing but don't. Saving for retirement. Avoiding the sun. Driving carefully. Driving less. Swearing off trans fats. It's not that I don't want to do these things; it's that I haven't figured out how to fully commit to them without losing my mind.

A working mom I know confirms that we all make choices. We let things go. If she had more time, she says, "My photo albums would be up to date, shaving would be a daily (not semi-monthly) event, and my 'to-be-filed' pile would not be skimming the ceiling." Notice she didn't mention flossing.

"It seems like taking care of myself is the first thing to go when it comes to balancing work and kids," says another working mom. "Simple things like flossing and washing my face at the end of the day seem like too much effort."

Perhaps the lesson is that our lives are over-scheduled. If we can't find time for basic personal hygiene, we're probably misprioritizing something. And maybe there's a smidgen of rebellion in our refusal to do the little things we know we should. There are so few responsibilities we grown-ups can let slide without facing serious consequences: poverty, prison, heart disease.

So if I can haul my kisser into the dentist twice a year while continuing to earn paychecks, maintain friendships, and raise a family, that'll have to be good enough.

Besides, if I can keep a colony of gum-dwelling bacteria alive and happy, it's more than I can say for my houseplants.

Sex Drive?

PUTTING THE BRAKES ON 'PARKING'

THERE ARE LOTS of things I used to enjoy in high school but don't now. Wine coolers. Sonic Youth. Amusement park rides that spin around in circles.

I recently had a revelation about another former pastime and was surprised at how suddenly, and strongly, it struck me: I never again want to get naked in an automobile. I was out on a date with my husband — sorry, honey — when the notion hit me. We'd seen a movie, had dinner. But we couldn't go home yet because one or both of our children might still be awake and, as any parent knows, a date that ends in the 437th consecutive reading of *Goodnight, Gorilla* has no right being called a date at all.

So we sat in our car, wondering what to do next. Bewitched by the urgent amorousness that only the absence of one's children can conjure, my spontaneous spouse glanced at the back seat, eyebrows raised. And before diplomacy could intervene — before I had fully processed the proposal, even — I heard myself say, "Yeah ... I think I'm all done with that."

The decision, I explained, was not personal but practical. Though I once derived a girlish thrill from the chaos of a mosh pit, or the incongruous texture of beach sand in my bed sheets, such disorder now chafes my grown-up sensibilities.

Besides, hanky-panky in a hatchback requires a flexibility of both mind and body that, frankly, I haven't been able to claim since the first Lollapalooza. No one looks alluring with her hair caught in a seat belt buckle, and I'm sorry but you can't call it "sexual freedom" if you're surrounded on all sides by upholstery. The dimensions give a whole new meaning to tuck and roll.

Car copulation, one of my girlfriends points out, is rarely an act of unbridled lust and more often the desperate act of a couple with literally no place else to go.

"I have not had sex in a car since the first day I had a key to my own dorm room," says the married mother of two. "The idea just doesn't appeal to me."

We haven't gone frigid, mind you. Meet us in the shower. Lead us to the rooftop. Clear off the kitchen counter, if you dare.

"I opt for hotels, motels, tabletops, heck even a chair," says another mom I know. "Just don't make me go back-seating again!"

Because the aversion is philosophical, too. When you're young and testing out your sexual potency, you want to know your partner will disrobe for you anywhere, at any time. But when your mutual attraction is well established

— and you're seeking sexual satisfaction, not just proof of your hotness — then you want something different from your guy: You want to know he'll wait until you're relaxed, reclined and (apologies to the squeamish) within 30 feet of a sink.

"Never say never," argues a particularly frisky — and, I should mention, newlywed — friend of mine. "And say 'Cadillac!' Making love in the back seat of a Cadillac is at least as comfortable as doing it on the couch."

But if car sex is a rite of passage, then perhaps giving it up is, too. A friend of mine with grown children recalls her own four-wheeled flings with fondness — but is equally happy to trade them in for the luxury of a later model.

"As one gets older, one must cultivate a more enchanted fantasy life," she says. "I'm frequently Ava Gardner on the beach with some young thing — a scene from *Night of the Iguana.*

"And I don't have to get the sand off my butt anymore."

Mop Scene

COMING CLEAN ABOUT HOUSEKEEPER GUILT

OH, GOD. Here she comes again. She's mopping now.

The housekeeper's here and — just as I was three Thursdays ago, and will be again three Thursdays from now — I'm utterly crippled with middle-class guilt.

I realize that ours is a consensual relationship: She agrees to scour my home and I agree to pay her good money so I don't have to. In theory, it's win-win. But there's something about the sight of this good-natured woman slogging up my stairs with her cleanser-filled bucket that just feels wrong.

The sound of her rigorous scrubbing ... the melancholy hum of her vacuum ... the chemical lemon scent ever-attempting to mask the caustic smell of servitude ... make it stop!

It's hard to maintain a respectful employer-employee relationship with someone who confronts your toenail clippings and empty Tylenol PM bottles on a regular basis. It's even more awkward because I work at home and have to lift my feet when she comes sweeping under my desk, clearing out dog hair, cookie crumbs and pen caps I didn't even know were down there.

I always consider leaving the room when she does this, both to make her job easier and to avoid the thought bubble above her head that says, "She doesn't look so busy. Why isn't she sweeping her own floor?"

Instead I stay put, to prove the point that what I'm doing here at this computer while she swipes cobwebs from my chandelier and bends over to dust my baseboards (Was that a grunt? Did she just actually grunt?) is hugely important work. Super vital stuff. Crucial.

I let out exaggerated stress-sighs once in a while, so she knows that while my work is not exhausting, nor does it smell bad, nor does it leave my fingernails a shambles, it does require deep contemplation. And a thesaurus. Plus I type really fast when she's in the room.

"Wow," she's probably thinking, "anyone who types that fast must be doing something very demanding, ponderous and of great import to society. I'm sure glad I don't have to sit on my butt all day and string sentences together for a living. Me, I'd rather be chiseling the soap scum out of some stranger's shower grout ... "

I should be flogged with a Swiffer, I really should.

It's not that I'm above cleaning, or that I'm too smart, skilled or snobbish for the task. It's that I suck at it. Truly. If a surface can't be rendered spotless with a Lysol wipe, I'm genuinely flummoxed and inclined to let it be until the next remodel.

But what bothers me most about the housekeeper quagmire is I feel like I'm dissing the sisterhood — the one established back when humans lived tribally. Women kept house collectively, sharing in the jobs of floor-sweeping, pelt-mending and acorn-grinding. So why is there currently a woman alone in my bathtub, high on Ajax?

I deserve to be tied down and have 409 dripped onto my forehead until I slowly go mad.

I can't help wonder: Is mine the filthiest house she encounters all month? Does she chide me to her friends and even her other clients? Do you think she calls me "Mrs. Dirty"?

The next time she stands beside my desk with her mop clicking, I want to face her and say, "We are not so unlike, you and me. We are both doing what we can to make a living. We both want respect for the things we're good at. And we both deserve to do our jobs with dignity."

I probably won't, though. I'll probably just lift my feet.

Fertile Fashion

WOMEN DRESS BETTER WHEN OVULATING

ALL WOMEN HAVE a range of clothes in their closet: oversized sweatpants, stuffy business jacket, slinky sundress. We see these incongruous vestments as symbols of our feminine mobility — beaded, boatnecked, buttoned-up proof that we can sashay from the laundry room to the board room to the Viper Room with the mere tug of a curve-hugging zipper.

Leave it to science to burst our bubble. It turns out there's another reason we favor diversified wardrobes — a biological one, in fact. A recent study showed that women's style of dress changes throughout our menstrual cycles: We opt for more attractive outfits as we near ovulation, the time of the month when we're most fertile.

Published last month in the journal *Hormones and Behavior*, the UCLA study photographed 30 young women during ovulation, and again during the least fertile phase of their cycle. Then, in what the university's publicists are calling "a kind of scientific version of the Web site 'Hot or

Not,' " a panel of men and women were asked to choose the photo in which each woman looked more "attractive."

Sixty percent of the time — a majority researchers insist is "well beyond chance" — judges chose the photo taken during ovulation. The subjects tended "to put on skirts instead of pants, show more skin, and generally dress more fashionably" at their most fertile, according to lead author Martie Haselton. It's not clear from the name or the study whether Haselton is an ovulator or an inseminator, but the good professor said the research proves "our evolution, our biology is showing up in even the most modern of behaviors."

One woman wore loose-fitting jeans and clunky boots during her low-fertility photo, and a skirt and cardigan during ovulation. Other subjects wore lower necklines, fancier jewelry, lace trims, and, um, fringe while ovulating. I can't remember the last time fringe was considered "fashionable" but, hey, different strokes for different evolutionary beings.

Other animals flaunt their fertility in a variety of ways. Cats release pheromones. Chimpanzees experience an obvious swelling of the genitalia when in heat. Certain dairy cows will wrinkle their noses and curl their lips or, strangely, try to mount other cows. Women, it seems, simply accessorize. Scientists have long believed that humans "conceal" their ovulation, but if perfect strangers can pick up on fertility cues just by looking at a couple snapshots, Haselton's research may have proven otherwise.

On one level, I applaud the research. If Darwin's Galapagos finches can have a sweet mating song, why shouldn't we ladies have a frisky mating wardrobe? Besides, it's fun watching scientists try to quantify abstract notions like "fashion," and translate concepts like "bling" into journal-worthy language. (Haselton told the *Washington Post* that ovulating co-eds engage in "self-ornamentation through attentive personal grooming.")

On the other hand, the results are troubling. Women have worked so hard to leave our breeder image back in the cave; it's disconcerting to learn that even as we demand professional tenure and storm the political landscape Xena-style, biology would still have us flirting shamelessly, even subconsciously — and with fringe, no less.

Scientists aren't certain that ovulating women dress nicely merely to attract male mates. It could just be the result of a biochemical mood change.

But what if it is done purely to woo studs to our mating ground or, in this case, dorm rooms? If women are programmed to don frillier frocks on the days when we're most likely to conceive a child, what other man-pleasing behaviors might we engage in halfway through our menstrual cycles? Taking the day off work to fry up bacon and watch *Robocop* in our underwear? Picking a barroom fight with the Jagermeister girl?

Forget it, ladies. I say watch your calendar and keep your sweatpants handy. We've come too far to let a few tiny genes dictate when and how we switch into come-hither mode. Biology may be powerful, but it's no match for a modern gal with a closet full of options. And free will — unlike evolution, but very much like my favorite hoodie sweatshirt — is entirely reversible.

Doppeldressers

I MET AN EXCEEDINGLY pleasant woman last week. Bubbly. Friendly. Open. Chatting at a school event, we found we had much in common: kids in the same class, husbands who were off in the corner avoiding chit-chat, a staggering appetite for potluck. We bonded like Bazooka to the bottom of a ballet flat.

But I knew something she didn't know. I knew how close we came to being enemies. Because the skirt she was wearing, an offbeat green number with a playful bounce and a bewitching shimmer to it, was the very same skirt that was hanging in my closet as she and I exchanged grins and carpool tips. The very same garment I had been planning to wear that night until a last-second outfit overhaul. The very same ring of common pleated cotton that, had we both shown up in it and been forced to schmooze side by side for two humiliating hours, would have caused me to hate this lovely woman's insufferable guts.

Wow, that looks even more psychotic when you see it in print.

But it's not a reaction I had any control over; it's visceral. Doppeldressers, or fashion facsimiles, if you will, tear at the very fabric of a woman's self-esteem. When we see a lady driving the same car as ours, we feel a kinship with her: Hey! She likes what I like! When we discover a coworker lives in our neighborhood, we embrace the coincidence: Cool! You, too, gave up ocean views for a bigger backyard!

But catch a fellow party guest sporting our beloved newsboy cap, slouchy ankle boot, or — oh no, she di'n't! — our splurge-of-the-season sailor pants, and (I'll deny that I typed this, but) someone's going to wind up with a purse full of Diet Coke before the evening's through.

To wit: "I wore a really cool coat to see George Clooney at the Santa Barbara International Film Festival," offered a stylish and normally sweet girlfriend of mine, "and some b*%@# had on the same coat."

You don't have to unzip this copycat-yields-catfight phenomenon very far to see what's causing it. "We all want to be the one who looks the best in the outfit," my friend confessed. Never mind if most of the women at the party already look better than us anyway; we seem to think that without the visual cue of identical outfits, no one will think to compare us. See, we were pulling off this taffeta bubble dress just fine before we met our "match," and now that fellow guests can see both of us in the same field of vision, it's distressingly clear that we had no business buying it in the first place and who exactly were we hoping to fool?

I'd like to blame *Us Weekly* for fostering this paranoid comparaphobia among sister-strangers. The glossy gossip rag — the same one known for its hard-hitting celebrity-cellulite exposés, mind you — runs an item called "Who Wore It Best," which juxtaposes the photos of two identically frocked starlets and asks readers to vote for who's cuter.

But in truth, women were stressing over show-stealing skirt burglars long before *Us* began running its invasive, demeaning, and thoroughly irresistible photo feature. Our aversion to duplicate dressers goes beyond "Who Wore It Best." It's about individuality, self-expression, and the immense satisfaction — indeed, validation — that comes from hunting down, finding, and then (yippee!) slipping into a truly unique item of clothing. Something with character. Something that makes you feel like yourself, only with the volume turned way, way up.

So it's only natural we should be miffed and disoriented when we spy a similarly clad floozy, er woman, expressing herself in our territory.

My new friend and I remain chummy. I'm choosing to cherish our similar taste rather than curse it. And I hope that's the way she'd see it, too, if she were in my shoes. Which she'd better never be.

Go With the Flow

THERE WERE GIRLS at my school who got their first period — and the almost-breasts that came with it — at age 11. We "late bloomers" revered them as divine othergirls, elevated beings with a god-given head start into grown-up-ness.

We would never catch up.

And yet, I was in no hurry to bleed. If it meant carrying a purse, wearing a bra and having to listen to "More Than a Feeling" while making out with Jamie Lieberman behind the handball court, then — gross — you could keep your lousy period.

The day it finally came, I threw up.

My parents took me out to dinner to "celebrate," and the stupid look on my father's face made me wonder if every single person in the family-style restaurant could tell I had gone from child to child-bearer that afternoon in the time it took me to finish my math homework.

When we got home, my meal leapt from my throat into

the very commode that had carried my first menstrual blood away just a few hours earlier. I felt like I couldn't keep anything of value inside me — like a rowboat that had sprung two simultaneous leaks.

Mom blamed the incident on a bad batch of soup, but I knew better. I knew it was my body chucking up the now defunct substructure of my senselessly slaughtered girlhood.

Either that, or it was the thought of kissing Jamie Lieberman.

I'm not the only girl who resisted climbing aboard the Womanhood Welcome Wagon.

"I was totally mortified," a friend of mine says about her first period. "I wasn't all proud and wanting to show it off like in a Judy Blume book — I just wanted it to go away."

Her grandma sent her a panty liner in the mail, "like a prize or something."

Another friend remembers her first visit from Aunt Flo: It was the very first day of summer vacation, and her plans to join friends at the beach were ... um ... soiled when her mother strapped her into a cumbersome sanitary belt — the kind no bikini can hide.

"I was miserable," she said. "There was nothing magical or womanly about it. It just sucked."

But wait. Hold the Midol. What if our periods didn't have to be so humiliating? What if American girls were as thrilled to get their first period as they are to get their first car? What if, as in other cultures, we could appreciate the changes that bleeding brings, rather than abhor them?

Local poet and playwright Lisa Citore poses such what-ifs in her new ensemble piece, *Bloodlines*. The show combines sensual dance and *Vagina Monologues*-style sketches for a mélange of menstrual musings as bold and unapologetic as a crimson stain on a once-pristine pair of white panties.

Citore, a cervical cancer survivor and sacred sexuality expert (whose invented surname spells "erotic" backwards), was inspired to write the play when her own daughter came of age recently.

The play goes a bit "woo woo" at times, insisting our genitals are a "holy portal," likening our sexuality to pomegranates and generally frightening those of us priggish pragmatists who have yet to be formally introduced to our wild inner goddesses. But it's also compelling, intriguing, strangely satisfying and uproariously funny in spots.

I'm taking some girlfriends to the show because my 248th moon is fast approaching. And if I've learned anything from two dozen years of sacred-if-vexing blood cycles, it's that laughter — the kind that gives your uterus a good jostling — is a fabulous cure for cramps.

A Gal in the Guys' Gym

I HAVE BEEN THRUST, Spandex-clad, into a world of sweaty, grunting beefcakes. And I don't like it as much as you'd think.

I've always enjoyed working out in the segregated sector of my gym: the walled-in "Women's Gym," a sunlit sanctuary for the sports-bra set. Here, floor-to-ceiling windows provided treetop views and frosted glass panes separated us from the facility's sprawling — and somewhat intimidating — gender-neutral weight room.

For a place devoted to fat-burning, our room was surprisingly comfy: It felt more like someone's living room, with gossip mags lying around, than a place to pump iron.

The real beauty of the all-girl fitness scene is going utterly unnoticed. No creeps to ogle us. No hunks to distract us. No reason to care if our butts really have no business in those stretch pants.

Sure, one of the reasons I exercise is to attract the

admiring eye of the opposite sex. But just as I wouldn't want that one hot Pilates teacher to see me wriggling into a Wonderbra or plucking my eyebrows, I don't need fellas gawking (or giggling) at me as I attempt to bulk up my chicken arms.

I'll proudly flaunt the outcome of my strength training, but the process should be private. It's personal. It's where the magic happens.

And the magic no longer happens in the Women's Gym. I arrived recently to find our machines relocated to a tiny, windowless room down the hall and our spacious former haven filled with bikes for Spinning.

Perhaps you're thinking, as I was, that if a person wants to perspire and pedal with a view of the outdoors, they ought to maybe *go ride a bike somewhere.*

In any case, my happy little workout bubble was popped. Doing squats in the cramped new room, with its clear glass wall between us and the surrounding gym, I felt like the star of a peep show. And I'm not one of those people who can pull off a great striptease in Reeboks.

So I stepped out of my comfort zone and into the foreign landscape of unisex-ercise. A place where the televisions thump and flicker with vulgar rap videos instead of Regis and Kelly. Where no one except me is reading a bright red pansy-ass paperback called *Five Men Who Broke My Heart.* Where men with bulbous triceps, swollen chests, and no sense of embarrassment grunt loudly as they hoist barbells the size of automobiles over their bulging heads.

If exercise hurts, I don't do it. And the gals in the Women's Gym seemed to understand that instinctively.

We shared an unspoken tenet: If you drag your glutes out of bed and muster the confidence to leave the house in Lycra, who really cares if you do four reps or 40? And hell, who's counting?

Not so in the wuss-free zone, where I am afraid to mount several machines (does one "mount" these things?) for fear a padded arm or steel bar will snap back and coldcock me. No one wants to be laughed at by people who are in far better shape than them.

There was a moment on the abductor machine when I thought I might learn to love this co-ed weight room. The equipment's better. It's less crowded. And I actually push myself to work harder knowing there are glistening fitness studs looking at me.

But then I realized something depressing: No one actually is looking at me. Not a single grunting beefcake. Hello? Female here!

So I think I'll limp back to the diminished Women's Gym. It's one thing to go unnoticed. It's another to be outright ignored.

Designer Vaginas

IF IT WEREN'T for my girlfriends, I would know nothing.

Over delicate lunches and sloppy happy hours, they keep me abreast of life's juicy tidbits: which teachers are retiring and which couples divorcing, which restaurants are closing and which movies opening.

But my gal pals caught me off guard recently when they told me about a freaky new nether-trend. I was biting into an overpriced burger downtown when one of my diva dining companions let this rip:

"Ever heard of a labe trim?"

Surely I had heard her wrong; I demanded clarification.

"Getting snipped. Down there. You know ... to make it ... neater."

She could have at least waited 'til I was finished chewing.

Indeed, the latest trend in cosmetic surgery has women spending thousands of dollars to have their most sensitive, most delicate regions re-sculpted, plumped up, liposuctioned, or nipped and tucked to look, um, prettier.

Statistics show "designer vaginas" are on the rise, with promising names to describe every peculiar procedure. Los Angeles doc David Matlock peddles vaginal "rejuvenation," aiming to restore a youthful "architectural integrity" to the female hoo-hah. Other surgeons hawk "revirgination" — a hymen reconstruction that allows women to feel (for what, one night?) like they're brand spankin' new again. (If memory serves, I'll pass.)

Lumped under a term that I must confess is my favorite new word — "vaginoplasty" — these procedures make up the fastest growing form of plastic surgery in the country. More than 1,000 women had cosmetic procedures on their coochies last year, according to the American Society of Plastic Surgeons. Gossip rags report that adult film actress Jenna Jameson had "work" recently (although it was reportedly botched, and complications can include infection and [gulp] loss of sensation).

It's understandable that a porn superstar might need an overhaul on her moneymaker from time to time. I can even see how a mother of four might require some doctoring to restore her parts to their once-perky configuration. (As a matter of fact, let's all do a kegel exercise right now, together. Okay, good.)

But what of the housewives and yoga instructors — and, yes, teenagers — who go under the knife because they are convinced their vulvas are just funny looking?

Sawbones who specialize in lily-gilding insist they do it to "empower" women, but critics question whether our power really lies in the relative length and symmetry of our genital folds.

My girlfriends and I weren't so much concerned with the politics of said surgery, but with the personal implications.

"How deliriously happy would you have to be with the rest of your body to put that on top of your plastic surgery fantasy list?" cracked one friend. "Let's see, I have rock solid abs, cellulite-free glutes, my boobs are up around my neck, but if you could just take an inch off the sides, that would be great."

Furthermore, none of us were curious — or limber — enough to have more than a passing idea of our own layout. And none had ever met a man whose sheer elation at a vaginal encounter could be dampened by even the gravest of aesthetic discord.

So why the fuss over shapely va-jay-jays? I blame Internet porn. With easy access to graphic images of Brazilian-waxed, barely legal, Photoshopped females — and who among us hasn't perused such material once or twice, while waiting for our bagel to toast? — our collective idea of what's "normal" is terribly skewed. Plastic surgeons say many of their patients come in for a consultation with a Playboy centerfold as a reference picture.

The antidote, of course, is to spend less time gazing at the modern media's images of "perfection," and more time yakking with our girlfriends. They may shock you sometimes — and even squelch your appetite — but if there's one thing gal pals are good for, it's assuring you that your labia are perfect just the way they are.

Love Bites

**WHEN THE MAN'S AWAY,
SCARF SPECIAL K**

SHE PAN-FRIES WITH PURPOSE, char-broils with cheer and grills with a Calphalon grin. She's the merry meal-maker, ever disposed to whip up a hot and hearty supper for her grumbling-tummied groom.

When he's home for dinner, she'll toast the bread, salt the beans, trim the steak and chill the salad — because that's the way he likes it best. She'll bust out the good napkins and soil every pan in the kitchen just so he can enjoy a "proper" meal. The kind his mommy used to make.

But tomorrow, when he's working late, she'll stand at the kitchen counter plucking almonds from the trail mix and polishing off her kids' leftover yogurt while thumbing through the junk mail.

And she'll take an impish thrill in doing it.

In 1814, American statesman John Adams wrote, "The shortest road to men's hearts is down their throats" (not to be confused with the Pillsbury Doughboy's syrupy insistence that "Nothin' says lovin' like somethin' from the oven"). Two centuries later, married women still heed the advice, going to far more trouble to feed our fellas than we ever would ourselves. Or our kids.

When their hubbies aren't home, my girlfriends delight in calling the following "dinner": Hot dog in a tortilla. Bowl of cereal with glass of wine. Hunk of cheese. Handful of grapes. Scoop (amen, sister) of cookie dough.

I used to think women like these — who slave over stoves for their spouses but settle for pantry snacks when they're alone — were submitting to sexism, relenting to patriarchy. Were they not worth the same effort as their hairy-legged household counterparts?! But as I sit here solo, sucking on a spoonful of peanut butter and seriously considering taking a fork to some cold, abandoned ravioli at the back of the fridge, I admit I was wrong.

There are lots of reasons women don't bother peeling carrots and pounding cutlets for ourselves — but low self-worth is not one of them.

Efficiency is. Like MacGyver on estrogen, we take an almost perverse pride in our ability to make a meal of, say, six frozen peas, some crackers and the last egg in the carton. We wouldn't ask our loved ones to eat it, you understand, but if we can fuel ourselves and free up a few Tupperwares, well, the evening's already been a success no matter if *Grey's Anatomy* is a repeat or not.

Convenience is another reason we eschew oven mitts when dining alone. Why scrub the wok when a bag of microwave popcorn is such a wealth of fiber? Plus women and men have different tastes; when we're not catering to their yen for gut-warming grub, we're free to graze as we like.

"I love to eat a salad for a meal when no one is demanding their meat-n-taters," admits a friend of mine, a mother of three. "Also, I see it as an opportunity to cut a few calories where I can."

If grazing is so superior to traditional table dining — cleaner, more practical, less fattening — why bother fixing "square" meals for our mates at all?

Because they really, really like it. If a man can no longer spend the day hunting an animal and having the satisfaction of seeing it on his plate that night, at least he can sit down to a meal that equals, if only abstractly, the hard work he logged at, um, the car lot.

"Guys don't 'require' a hot meal any more than women 'require' our lawns to be clipped and our car oil to be changed," says another mom I know, who goes on cooking strikes when her husband leaves town. "But they like having someone take care of the things they may not excel at, just like we do."

Maybe the damned Doughboy knows his romance after all.

Everything I Know About Men I Learned at Strip Clubs

WHILE IN PORTLAND, ORE., for a journalism conference last week, I boarded a rumbly old school bus for a tour of the city's all-nude strip clubs. The bus was crowded, as good journalists never miss the chance to peek into a furtive subculture or, it turns out, to look at boobies.

Visiting five burlesque clubs in one night was a whirlwind education, but even more fascinating than the stage acts was the clientele. While men in buttoned-down shirts and loafers fixated on the gyrating sirens before them, I watched the watchers. Because when you strip away the pretense of dating and the art of romance, you get a little titillating insight into the male mating psyche — the naked truth, if you will.

1) It's different strokes for different blokes.

Most guys will tell you a strip club is like pizza. When it's good, it's really, really good. And when it's bad... well, it's still pretty good.

But different dancers appeal to different fellas. Some guys on our bus fell hard for a surgically enhanced coquette in a schoolgirl get-up. Others swooned over a 6-foot-tall beach bunny whose Barbie-like proportions compensated for her lethargic undulating. Still others were enchanted by a tattooed, mohawked minx named Malice.

Small breasts and large. Short hair and long. Leather and lace. After a few bump-and-grind numbers, my friend Michelle and I were bored.

"You seen one," she deadpanned, "you seen 'em both."

But the men disagreed, gleefully dedicating themselves to the time-consuming task of finding their stripping soul mate, and lavishing her with a tender "WOOOOO-HOOOOOOO!!!!!" once they did.

2) *Men appreciate fastidious grooming.*

It would be unfair to say all men like their strippers shaved bald where it counts. But of the dozen-plus dancers we saw that night, nary a one of them had the hair God gave a hamster. No tidy triangle. No artful landing strip. Just a whole lotta bare there.

Strippers build their acts — their appearance, moves, and music — around tips, and if they're going for the 10-year-old girl look, it's because that's what brings in the greenbacks.

I'm willing to entertain the idea that men fling money at these waxed-to-the-navel girls because they feel sorry for them — you know, because they look cold. But until it's confirmed, can we all at least agree that Puritanism has worked some funky voodoo on our nation's sexual soul?

3) Men need, um, guidance.

Here is consolation for any woman who's had trouble keeping a man's focus on a dinner date: One stripper told me dancers routinely slap their thighs or click their high-heeled shoes together to draw customers' attention back to the stage. And they're naked.

4) Men are not fussy.

The women in our group were impressed by contortionists who could knot their legs behind their backs and by gymnasts who spun around their poles, upside-down, by their ankles. That's talent.

But such artistry was wasted on the guys, whose singular criterion for a successful striptease was — and you gotta love their candor — an unobstructed view of the goods.

5) Men make lousy strippers — I don't care how gay they are.

For variety's sake, Michelle and I abandoned the tour and took a cab to a gay strip club, where beautiful men posed in cages wearing just Speedos and smiles.

We didn't find them all that arousing, in part because they just sort of stood there flexing their grins, and in part because what turns on men is very different from what turns on women.

That said, if you know of a bus tour that showcases men who can make a woman laugh while hammering something and, say, packing their kids' lunches, please sign me up.

A Week of Strong

It is Monday, and I am a testament to human discipline. I am will power incarnate.

Last weekend, like all weekends before it, I was confronted with a barrage of shame-inducing images: Fleshless twenty-somethings flitting along downtown sidewalks in jeans tighter than the skin on grapes. Itty bitty bikinis dangling in department store windows, looking more like polka dot rubber bands than something that might actually cover my ba-donk-a-donk. And a magazine ad featuring a plate of sweet 'n' sour pork that was supposed to warn me about the dangers of high cholesterol, but just made me really, really hungry. All of which inspired me toward a Sunday night resolution: to procure a sleeker silhouette, a bikini-ready bod, through sheer self-control. I begin today.

For breakfast, I eat three spoonfuls of plain oatmeal, which I can tell is extremely healthy because it tastes like wet bread. I attend a Pilates class, where the chipper teacher seems annoyed by my loud whimpering and refusal to do any push-ups (doesn't that seem like a task best left to more experienced students?). I nibble carrot sticks all day. I chug water to purge the toxins left by too many Circus Animal cookies in my previous, feeble-willed existence.

"I AM resolute. I CAN have six-pack abs if I want them. I WILL treat my body like the temple that it is."

It is Tuesday. Am I imagining it or are my workout pants looser? I sweeten my oatmeal with Splenda and set out on a two-mile walk. I stop at Starbucks and treat myself to a fat-free cappuccino and muffin (a gross one with bran and dried fruit, so don't lecture me).

Tonight's affirmation: "I AM pretty studly. I CAN picture myself in a polka dot rubber band. I WILL pick up a tube of that Dove Firming Lotion, just to supplement my other efforts."

It is Wednesday and I am in pain. Ow. Damn those Pilates. It hurts when I slather firming lotion on my stomach, thighs, butt, upper arms, and the sort of jowly thing under my chin. It even hurts when I carry the big bag of chocolate chips to the table to sprinkle a few on my oatmeal. I opt for a workout video at home and grunt through a few squats and squeezes. Then I switch over to the E! channel instead so I can flick carrot sticks at Teri Hatcher and Keira Knightley and tell them how I feel sorry for them because they don't have any curves, and so I really wonder how they'll ever snag a man.

Affirmation: "I AM not 22 anymore. I CAN accept that dieting is not my forte. I WILL have to pick up all the errant carrot sticks in the living room as soon as I can bend over freely again."

It is Thursday and I'm freaking starving. I actually taste the firming lotion. I don't feel like exercising. I drive to Starbucks, parking at the far end of the lot so I can get my heart rate up before I suck down a full-fat cappuccino and muffin. OK, it's not a muffin, it's a cupcake. But I save half of it for later. Only I wind up eating it in the car on the way home.

"I AM entitled to a day off from my fitness regimen. I CAN take a break without backsliding into sloth and gluttony. I WILL begin again tomorrow, refreshed and recommitted."

It is Friday and screw the oatmeal, I'm just having the chocolate chips today — with a chaser of Circus Animal cookies. I picture the face of that Pilates tyrant as I bite their little heads off and cackle. I have no intention of breaking a sweat today, unless it's to dog-paddle through a pool of firming lotion.

"I AM done with this nonsense. I CAN always just buy a bigger bathing suit. I WILL be ordering sweet 'n' sour pork before Monday rolls around again ... when I'm due back at Pilates."

Watch Her Strut

LONG HAVE MEN made a hobby of studying women's wiggles. Dale Hawkins liked the way his Susie Q swaggered in the '50s. In the midst of his 1979 hit "Here Comes My Girl," Tom Petty erupted in a growly "Watch her walk!" Jane Fonda's girlish gait inspired Bob Seger to pen the roadhouse grinder "Her Strut": "They do respect her, but ... they love to watch her strut." (Or perhaps it's: "They do respect her butt. They love to watch her strut." Either way, really.)

Now researchers in Europe have turned men's perambulation-peeping pastime from an art into a science. A recent study published in the *Journal of Sexual Medicine* showed that just by watching a woman walk, experts could predict her ability to have vaginal orgasms (as opposed to clitoral orgasms, which sticklers consider to be cheating but which, for the record, most women still prefer over a dozen roses).

Researchers at the University of the West of Scotland

had a sampling of young women answer questions about their sexual history. Then they videotaped the ladies walking through a public place and asked a couple of "trained sexologists" to watch the tape and guess which ones were prone to vaginal orgasms. Let's pause here while our male readers kick themselves for going into the wrong line of work.

These esteemed professors of sexology guessed right more than 80 percent of the time, insisting that the subject's stride length and vertebral rotation was greater for the vaginally orgasmic women. In layman's terms, the climax-tending gals are just more loosey-goosey.

"This could reflect the free, unblocked energetic flow from the legs through the pelvis to the spine," the authors noted. Or, they confessed, it could just be that women who get a rockin' release every now and again have more spring in their step.

But maybe there's a better explanation, as one reader on a news site (physorg.com/news) suggested: "Perhaps these women walk with a gait that attracts men who 'know how to please a woman'?"

Another post implied that the sexy walk/satisfied lover correlation is already common knowledge — and common sense. "It's no secret," she wrote, "except to academics. And we all know how most of them walk."

In my experience, a cowgirl's trot has less to do with her yeehaw than her boots. Birdlike baby steps, for example, don't mean a lady's hard to please; it means she gets cheap, even dirty, thrills from platform heels and pencil skirts.

And a bombshell with a jazz-club bounce — you know, the kind of swishing saunter where her hips jut out to the right and left, snapping crisply before being slung to the other side, the kind of sway that makes you hear the brush of a high-hat with each sultry step — isn't a sure thing, either. She's probably just ecstatic over the squish of her Strappy Strips insoles.

In truth, it's hard to fathom how this orgasm study might prove useful. The researchers say a potential link between muscle blocks and sexual function could improve women's sex lives. And who am I to shuffle, amble or even trip into the path of progress?

But one has to wonder whether the entire experiment was just an excuse to grill a group of young students about their sex lives and then — as Hawkins, Petty, and Seger did before them — check out their cha-chas.

The theory becomes ever more plausible when you consider the study's paltry sample size: 16 Belgian coeds.

"Oh, they do respect her, but ..."

Talula Does the Hula From Hawaii

YOU'LL NEVER MEET a child named Sex Fruit in New Zealand. Nor will you make the acquaintance of Fat Boy, Stallion or Cinderella Beauty Blossom.

The nation's government blocked all of these names, and earlier this year allowed a 9-year-old girl to change her name from the one her parents gave her:

Talula Does the Hula From Hawaii.

"It makes a fool of the child and sets her up with a social disability and handicap," said the ruling judge.

I don't disagree that the name is absurd, but ... disability? The story sparked comments on countless blogs, where readers lashed out at parents who "cruelly" saddle their offspring with offbeat names.

But I have to tell you: It's not as bad as everyone thinks.

With the exception of Talula, few names are sillier than mine. It comes from the song "Good Morning, Starshine" from the 1960s musical *Hair*, in which my dad starred. Between you and me, it's a stupid song, but it was an important moment in our nation's culture and my family's history.

People mistakenly assume I was teased mercilessly as a child. The fact is kids are immature about everything; they'll make fun of a Jack (in the box) or a (plain) Jane just as gladly as they'll poke fun at a Tiger or Venus. And being fairly new to the world, children don't assume Apple is any weirder than Elizabeth — at least Apple's a word they've heard before.

Adults sometimes react rudely to my name, but I've learned it's more a reflection of their own discomfort and (how to put this?) narrow life experience than a "disability" on my part.

That said, we oddly-named folks do have some issues. I flat-out refuse to spell my name for anyone. It's irrational, but if I have to overcome airhead stereotypes and smile politely when people call me Skylight, I have little patience left for strangers who can't sound out a simple compound word.

My friend Skye and I both have trouble remembering other people's names because, during introductions, we're so focused on explaining our own that we forget to concentrate on theirs.

Still, we all love our unique names. "A little ribbing from your peers builds character," insists my friend Seraphim.

We tend to grow into the names our parents give us, like my friend Happy, the grinningest guy I know, with a sense of humor to match. "Fortunately," he says, "I was never confused with the other six dwarves."

The worst part about a quirky name is you can't find it pre-printed on those mini-license plates they sell at tourist shops. And the best part is the foregone conclusion that you're special.

"My name led to the early realization that there is nobody like me," says my colleague Starre. "And that's pretty awesome."

Most of us think it's such a blessing, we want our kids to share it. "I would hesitate before giving a child a 'normal' name," says my girlfriend Arcadia, whose daughter is Luna. "I don't want to perpetuate mediocrity."

Neither did my friend Linda. "As a child," she says, "I had an artistic soul and always hated how bland and common my name was." She named her son Chance and says he doesn't get teased — but then his buddies are Trip, Doc and Blade.

Who knows how those names would fare in New Zealand, or Sweden, where moms and dads have landed in court for calling their kids Lego, Ikea and Metallica. Last year, Venezuela considered adopting a list of 100 "acceptable" names that parents could legally choose from.

My atypically tagged friends and I are glad the United States has no law preventing parents from calling junior whatever they want.

"If they want to name him X, they can name him X," says the woman who answers the phone at Santa Barbara County Health Statistics.

Sounds good to me. At least he wouldn't have to spell it.

Obama, Sweetie

TERM OF ENDEARMENT LEAVES BITTER AFTERTASTE

HERE'S THE TRUTH: I'm sweet on Barack Obama, and the man can call me whatever he wants as long as he doesn't let that war-mongering glad-hander into our White House. No, not Hillary. The other one.

But last week the likely Democratic nominee said something that left a bitter taste in some Americans', um, ears: He called a journalist "sweetie."

During a Detroit factory tour, a TV reporter asked how Obama planned to help autoworkers, and the senator said, "Hold on, sweetie, we'll do a press avail," meaning he'd make time for questions soon.

In fact, he never did answer the very legit question, or make time for others. And what most peeved the press was not his evasion. It was his condescending remark — a word he had also lobbed at a Pennsylvania factory worker just last month.

Barack, baby! Honey! Sugarlips! This ain't no way to

win Clinton's bra-sporting supporters.

As a woman, and a reporter, I can tell you there's little that chafes the patience like being addressed — in a professional setting — with the same patriarchal smarm you'd use to charm a waitress at a pie shop off the interstate.

Actor Jimmy Smits called me sweetheart once during an interview — you know, in that smooth-as-cream voice of his — and I instantly hated him. Still do. I don't care how high your cheekbones are, or how much better you looked in the nude than Dennis Franz; sexist banter is a turn-off. And my reaction to it was visceral.

But why? This is not the worst thing a man could say to a woman. It's not that thing McCain allegedly called his wife. Come to think of it, I'd rather be called sweetie than a lot of the names I've had beaned at me — many of which were well earned.

Most gals don't mind the label when it comes from, say, a doting dad. Or an elderly gentleman asking for a hand getting off the bus. But in most other settings, it's patronizing. It attempts to establish an ad-hoc gender hierarchy where none actually exists, and implies (here's where we bitches really bristle) that there's something adorable about a dame doing serious work. Getting in a candidate's face. Demanding answers.

That said, we can't condemn Obama without demanding some more answers: First, if female professionals are so tough, why would we let such a minor slight ruffle us? Second, if the senator had been walking with the reporter, and had stopped to hold a door open so she could pass through first, would he have been called chauvinistic or chivalrous?

Chromosomal carping aside, I'm not as depressed about his mistake as I am impressed with his response to it. When an aide pointed out the gaffe, Obama personally phoned the reporter and apologized — both for failing to field press questions and for speaking thoughtlessly.

"That's a bad habit of mine," Obama confessed of his sweetie slip. "I do it sometimes with all kinds of people. I mean no disrespect and so I am duly chastened on that front."

In the good-ole-boy culture of politics, it's not unusual for men to talk down to women. But it's rare for any politician, male or (ahem) Iraq War-voting female, to own up to stupid errors. And rarer still for them to do it eloquently.

Duly chastened? That, sweetie, is how you turn "sexist" into "sexy."

X Appeal

WHY ARE CELEBS STILL MAKING SEX TAPES?

THERE ARE NOT a lot of things we, as a society, can learn from Rob Lowe. The pretty-boy actor and Montecito resident can't teach us, for example, how to express genuine emotion in front of a camera. Or, for that matter, how to build our dream home without infuriating our neighbors.

But there's one valuable lesson we can glean from Rob Lowe's substantial life experience: If you're famous, for god's sake don't tape yourself having sex.

Earlier this month, when Kevin Federline found out wife Britney Spears was filing for divorce, he allegedly threatened to release a home sex video of them unless she awarded him millions of dollars and full custody of their two young sons. Because nothing says "responsible father" like extortion, and amateur porn.

K-Fed supposedly contacted celebrity smut salesman David Hans Schmidt to negotiate a price for the four-hour movie, which is said to show the tabloid darlings getting busy and — inexplicably — playing chess. I honestly don't know which I'd less rather see.

Spears countered Federline's threat by promising to release the video herself so that her ex couldn't leverage it against her. (Which implies there are copies of the tape. Were they planning to send them out as Christmas gifts?) Federline's attorney now insists his client never threatened to blackmail Spears and that, in fact, no such sex tape exists. Please.

She has gyrated with a snake, French-kissed Madonna, and posed nude for the cover of *Harper's Bazaar.* He compares himself to Jesus in his famously-panned music.

Together, they starred in UPN's reality series "Britney & Kevin: Chaotic," which subjected the world to hours and hours of the couple's tamer home movies.

Frankly, if this match-made-in-narcissistic-heaven hadn't aimed a 10x zoom lens at their marital bed and the famous flesh that flops around in it, I'd be stunned. What's surprising, though, is ... why?

Former Brat Packer Rob Lowe saw a sizeable career slump after he was discovered to have videotaped himself in Atlanta in 1988 having sex with two women, one of whom was underage. Around the same time, another video cropped up showing Lowe in a tawdry threesome in a Paris hotel room. Speaking of Paris, Miss Hilton's famous hardcore romp with former beau Rick Salomon made more than $50 million when distributed commercially against her will. Colin Farrell sued former Playboy bunny Nicole Narain for trying to make money off a tape of their X-rated escapades.

And who could forget the honeymoon video of Pamela Anderson and former hubby Tommy Lee that was allegedly stolen from their Malibu home only to become the year's most popular porn rental?

Pammy's new yet soon-to-be-ex hubby Kid Rock recently went to court to block the release of a tape of him and Creed frontman Scott Stapp getting friendly with groupies on a tour bus. (Was Rock, the author of such ditties as "Wax That Booty," worried he'd seem like a womanizer? Or did the tape reveal him to be a less, um, substantial lover than he'd have us believe?)

I have no problem with these folks seeking bare-bummed bliss on boats, buses, and in penthouse suites. I truly don't. My issue with them committing their copulation to celluloid is not that it's raunchy — it's that it's so very, very stupid.

I'm sure it seems like a harmless lark at the time. When most of your life is lived in front of a camera, it's easy to forget the inherent value of intimacy. And humility. But sooner or later, the tape always falls into the wrong hands, allowing the world to see what these folks look like when makeup artists aren't handy to powder their shiny parts. Despite movie posters, music videos, and millions of PR dollars spent touting them as unattainable sex machines, they're revealed to be run-of-the-mill Hollywood floozies who make embarrassing choices when intoxicated, and weird sounds during intercourse.

If the Spears tape ever makes it to the Internet, celebs should make a point of watching it. One glimpse will scare them off of hand-held cameras forever. If not, it's bound to improve their chess game.

Palin Comparison

THE HEIR A PARENT?

HERE ARE FIVE WORDS I never thought I'd type: Quit picking on the Republican.

Believe me, no one reviles the GOP more than I. No one is more resentful of the way — by spitting and sneering — they've made filthy epithets out of once-neutral words like "liberal," "homosexual," and "Muslim." No one gets queasier when the party's politicians cozy up to corporations and brandish Old Glory's broad stripes and bright stars in an effort to distract us from waxing fuel prices and waning civil liberties.

Excuse me while I swig some Pepto.

But ever since Senator John McCain named Sarah Palin his running mate, red and blue voters alike have been all a-chirp over the woman's qualifications. Not her qualifications for the vice presidency, mind you, but as a mother. Which doesn't sit well in the ol' gut, either.

How can she accept a nomination, they ask, that will cast intense scrutiny on her five kids, one of whom is a pregnant, unmarried teen? (Palin, though, was happy to drag her Army-enlisting son into the spotlight at last week's convention.) And didn't the would-be VP take an eight-hour flight home from Texas in April, after going into labor at a governor's convention? Isn't that irresponsible?

Santa Barbara's own Laura Schlessinger, a McCain supporter who has asked me never to call her for a quote, pooh-poohed Palin on her blog (drlaurablog.com): "What kind of role model is a woman whose fifth child was recently born with a serious issue, Down Syndrome, and then goes back to the job of governor within days of the birth?"

Let me be clear: I'm all for attacking Sarah Palin. Slam her for flip-flopping her position on Alaska's "Bridge to Nowhere." Deride her for the cheap, inaccurate jabs at Obama, and the smug "take that" mug she flashes when she lets them rip. And, for god's sake, if anyone's having a Smear the Beauty Queen party, I do hope you'll invite me.

But maligning her mamahood is out of bounds. Not because it's mean. Not because girls can't take the heat. And not even because no one ever asks how Dubya manages to juggle kids and a career (one assumes he doesn't and moves on, right?).

No, calling her parenting into question is remiss for one reason only: It's irrelevant.

While I have empathy for her kids, the truth is I don't care what kind of mother she is. While I'm proud to see a woman on the ticket, I don't care what kind of role model she is. Though I'm glad not to face the pressures she does, I don't care if she has trouble balancing her job and family.

I care what she plans to do about war, abortion, gay marriage, energy, and the environment. These are my issues. Surely everyone has something they can care about more than who'll knit booties for Bristol Palin's love child.

To be fair, I felt the same way about Bill Clinton: I wouldn't want to be married to the guy. Wouldn't even want to accidentally bump up against him at a backyard barbecue (okay, maybe a little). But damn if he wasn't an inspiring chief executive.

Look, we'd all like to believe that it takes a good person to be a good politician — that someone with values and even schedules like our own will best represent us in office. But deep down we know it takes something very different to succeed in Washington. A tough hide. A touch of idealism. A great poker face. And a knack for tracking, and even anticipating, the temperamental tides of power.

Maybe Sarah Palin has those qualities. Maybe she'd bring them — and her diaper bag — to the White House. I, for one, hope never to find out.

The Great Disney Smoke-Out

REMEMBER THE HOOKAH-PUFFING Caterpillar in *Alice in Wonderland?* The one whose cloudy exhalations made poor Alice cough, sputter and sneeze? His killer buzz just went up in smoke.

Disney president Robert Iger recently vowed to snuff out all depictions of smoking in the studio's future family films. He said the company recognizes its profound influence over children, and while entire generations have been misled into believing that charming princes will rescue helpless but pretty girls, and that we should all adopt the life philosophy of a shiftless singing meerkat, he wants them to also know that a drag on a Marlboro will kill you dead.

Or something to that effect.

I suspect the decision was, in part, a nod to the ghost of Walt Disney himself, a chain smoker who died of lung cancer in 1966.

Advocacy groups have been hard-pressuring

Hollywood to kick its on-screen smoking habit, and the Motion Picture Association of America announced in May that it would add smoking to the list of cinematic sins — including violence, profanity, nudity and drug use — that earn films harsher ratings.

Which is ironic, of course, when you consider the silver screen's Golden Age, during which stars like Bette Davis and Humphrey Bogart were rarely seen without a cig in their elegantly lit, black-and-white fingers.

But if you add up the admittedly disturbing numbers — 75 percent of youth-rated movies depict smoking, and 175,000 Americans die from lung cancer each year — Disney's decision makes both dollars and sense.

Sure, the ban is one of those wholly symbolic gestures that will benefit the studio more than any of its viewers. There never was much puffery in Disney properties to begin with: Cruella de Vil's long cigarette holder, Peter Pan's peace pipe. So an official smoke-out is a tiny effort to make in order to look like Hollywood heroes.

In some ways, the new policy is goofy. Iger's reasoning is that "cigarette smoking is a hazard." But so are sea witches, flying elephants and power-mad, hook-handed pirates. Disney films are full of behavior you wouldn't want your kids to emulate: driving like Mr. Toad, lying like Pinocchio or stealing like Robin Hood — a common thief despite his right-hearted empathy for the poor and his sexy (I'm sorry, but prrrr) vigilante persona. Is it irresponsible for Disney to romanticize the artery-clogging pasta binge in which Lady and her high-cholesterol Tramp so carelessly engage?

Ultimately, though, I don't want my kids lighting up any more than Bob Iger wants his stock dropping down. And since I've never bothered to complain that Disney flicks don't show unprotected sex between unmarried mermaids, or depict needle-sharing between HIV-postive forest dwarves, then I really can't lament the loss of realism when they choose to begin erasing other ugly habits from their otherwise immaculate scripts.

No, the problem isn't in Disney prissing up its kiddie flicks; it's in Iger's promise to make a "serious attempt to eliminate" smoking in the company's subsidiaries, Touchstone and Miramax. How would Miramax period films *Gangs of New York, Chicago* and *The Aviator* have looked with no cigarettes in them? How do you suppose Quentin Tarantino will react when they tell him that the characters in next year's planned World War II flick *Inglorious Bastards* can maim as many people as they want, but they'd better not blow a single smoke ring?

The director's bound to have some R-rated words for them, and I hope the movie-going public speaks up, too. Because when the Mouse House begins dictating which real-life behaviors grown-ups have a right to see — when cinema verite becomes cinema very-tame, and the exalting of squeaky clean role models becomes hazardous to my entertainment — then forgive me, Walt, but it's time for us all to pipe up.

Turning the Other Cheek on Spanking

THERE ARE TWO THINGS I know for sure about spanking:
    (1) It's wrong.
    (2) I've done it anyway.

Americans have an odd relationship with corporal punishment. On the one hand, we are an enlightened country that professes civil rights for all citizens. We don't allow business owners to beat their workers. We no longer tolerate husbands who wallop their wives. We even want reassurance that "no animals were harmed in the making of this film."

But on the other hand, we don't want anyone telling us how to raise our children. California lawmaker Sally Lieber felt the sting of this double-sided reasoning recently when she proposed a bill that would make it illegal for parents to swat their young children on the rump. Snarky late-night TV hosts mocked her. Traditionalists played the "How dare you?" card. Fellow legislators — including Democrats — refused to back the bill.

So Lieber proposed instead a narrower bill that would punish parents for hitting kids in the head, whacking them with a stick, whipping them with a belt — but would not interfere with a good, old-fashioned thwap on the tush. Hard to argue with a bill that basically reiterates existing laws against child abuse, but Lieber may come up short on votes. How can our government pinpoint the line between "cruel" and "justifiable" forms of discipline when many parents don't even know where it lies for us personally?

Sure we've come a long way from the rod-sparing, child-spoiling days when a good paddling was believed to "drive the devil out" of our young'uns. And while some families still believe spanking to be a reasonable, and even loving, way to teach self-control, we progressive moms and dads consider any form of corporal punishment to be archaic. Barbaric even. We like to quote Isaac Asimov, who said, "Violence is the last refuge of the incompetent."

"I really don't believe in spanking," proclaimed a friend of mine, a mother of two with a Mensa IQ. "But sometimes I feel like I have to because nothing else is working. I'm not proud of it."

"When my son was a baby, I remember thinking I would never touch my kids," added a guy I know, a Buddhist father of three. "Not long after, I slapped him on the face. I couldn't believe I'd crossed that line. But it can be very difficult to remember your own philosophy when your kids have driven you way, way, waaaaay past the point of utter exhaustion."

Lots of parents agree that a swift swat is reasonable punishment for a toddler who reaches for a hot stove or darts into traffic — namely, when we can't afford for an important safety lesson to be learned via natural consequences.

But hitting children to make them obedient? To earn their respect?

I've always thought parents who use spanking as a regular form of discipline — "premeditated spankers," you might call them — were cold-hearted. But is it really worse than slapping our children despite our beliefs? Are those of us who resort to it better parents than those who rely on it?

I spanked my 3-year-old once, after he'd spent the entire day lashing out in frustration: shoving my legs, throwing a toy at my head. When I announced it was bedtime and he slapped my face, I lost it. I turned him over and gave him a solid BAM! on the butt, muttering something absurd about how we don't hit in our house.

We were both shocked into tears, and I'm not sorry he learned how demoralizing it feels to be hurt by another human being — but I'm sorry he learned it from me.

More than anything, though, I regret the second lesson he learned that day, the one that was unintentional but surely packed more punch than the first: She with the stronger right hook wins.

I Now Pronounce You Sissy and Wife

IT'S WEDDING SEASON again, and that means half of every aisle-trodding couple will be struggling with the decision of whether to take on their spouse's last name or keep their own. But according to a new trend, it might not be the half you think.

The California Assembly passed a bill last week that, if adopted by the Senate and signed by the governor, will allow newly married men to change their last names as easily as women do. A bride needs only to fill out some forms and notify her credit card companies if she wants to take her husband's name. But a growing number of grooms — from Mike Davis-turned-Salinger in Seattle to Christopher Sclafani-turned-Rhee in Washington, D.C. — are opting to take their wives' last names instead, either to honor the women's heritage, preserve a family name that's at risk of dying out, upgrade to an easier-to-spell moniker, or simply do their small part to roll back centuries of gender inequity.

Current law requires these guys to spend hundreds of dollars, get permission from a judge, and wait several months to legally adopt a married name. Forward-thinking Los Angeles dude Michael Buday recently called No fair! on the process, prompting the ACLU to file a federal lawsuit and cosponsor the Name Equality Act on his behalf. Seven states — Hawaii, New York, Massachusetts, Iowa, Louisiana, Georgia, and North Dakota — already allow a husband to take a wife's name, and I can see why.

The married-name conundrum is a tricky one. Who wants to switch identities mid-career? Who wants to exchange one pronunciation nightmare for another? I didn't. But neither did my husband.

John and I had already been hitched two years when we decided, in 1996, that we wanted the same last name. We were about to buy our first home and figured the paperwork would be easier if our signatures matched. We planned to have kids and liked the idea of a common family identity. We relished the romance of being forever linked by letters, each of us a reflection on the other. And I could tell you it was those considerations that compelled us to do what we did — convenience, romance, and a nod toward our mutual future.

But in truth, it was the wine. Too much of the house red at a nearby trattoria convinced us the best way to honor our union was to combine our two distinct last names into one new one. Thus did my English Rowell and his bastardized French Gaushell morph — after reams of paperwork, published legal notices, courthouse visits, and scads of cash — into the acultural, unhistorical, but hard-to-mispronounce hybrid, Roshell.

We weren't trying to change the world. We were just trying to embody equity, regardless of the inconveniences it might bring. (And bring it did. His parents were furious, as you might imagine.)

Our solution to the married-name issue is not unheard of. Los Angeles Mayor Antonio Villaraigosa was Mr. Villar before marrying Corina Raigosa in 1987. But most forward-thinking couples still choose to keep separate last names, or hyphenate them. And the Lucy Stone League, an equality-promoting group named after a feisty female who refused to take her husband's name when she married in 1855, claims the vast majority of brides still drop their maiden names outright.

Will California's new law change that? Conservatives, of course, hope not. Most of the Assembly's Republicans voted against the bill, presumably because it would let domestic partners change their names, too — allowing gay couples to parade around with matching surnames just like us God-sanctioned married folks.

The right-wing Campaign for Children and Families group released a statement opposing the bill and saying, I kid you not, that the state shouldn't be encouraging its hubbies to be sissy men who abdicate their masculine leadership role because they're confused.

Hey. That's Mr. Sissy Man to you, buddy.

Cold-Hearted or Hot-Blooded?

PICK ONE.

We Americans want it all, don't we? Food that's cheap but delicious. Airports that are safe yet convenient. Presidents who are smart and still say damned charming things like "misunderestimated."

But time and again, we find we can't have it both ways.

Just look at our reaction to the plight of Lisa Nowak, the NASA astronaut who lost her boys' club cool last week and attacked a romantic rival with pepper spray.

While wearing a wig.

And, um, a diaper.

Police are calling it a love triangle: Nowak, a decorated Navy engineer who flew on the space shuttle Discovery in July, drove 12 hours from Houston to Orlando to confront Air Force Capt. Colleen Shipman, with whom she was competing for the affections of astronaut Bill Oefelein. She wore adult diapers so she wouldn't have to pull over at rest stops, disguised herself in a wig and trench coat, followed Shipman to her car and then sprayed her in the eyes with pepper spray before her victim escaped and got help.

Police found a BB gun in Nowak's car, along with a four-inch folding knife, gleaming steel mallet, latex gloves, four feet of rubber tubing, garbage bags and $600 cash.

Unless she planned to construct a crude getaway parachute — or a sophisticated diaper-disposal system — it all looks bad for Nowak.

Now the 43-year-old mother of three is facing charges of attempted murder while America blithely lampoons her as a wingnut. Headlines like "Lust in Space" and "Dark Side of the Loon" topped the news story. Jay Leno joked about the aerospace engineer being the worst sort of flight risk and David Letterman offered the "Top Ten Signs an Astronaut Is Trying to Kill You."

All of which is funny, indeed, and I'm not saying Nowak's sane. NASA's psychological screenings notwithstanding, I'd rather wander Fresno with Anne Heche's alien ego than sip Tang with this mallet-wielding galaxy trotter.

But isn't it hypocritical of us, as a nation, to mock a woman like Nowak for letting her heart guide her actions — when we revile Hillary Clinton for doing just the opposite?

The comparison between Captain Nowak and Senator Clinton may seem strained — one's running for President and the other, thanks to a court-mandated ankle bracelet, isn't running anywhere. But both women have attained a rare level of success in grace-under-pressure careers dominated by men. Nowak is known as "Robochick" for operating the space shuttle's robotic arm. As the less popular half of "Billary," Clinton was believed to have undue influence over her husband's presidency.

And both, now, have seen their professional achievements undermined by amorous entanglements. But if one of them horrifies the nation by hunting down the "other woman," and the other is labeled "cold-hearted" for sticking with her philandering spouse, there appears to be a double standard at work:

When successful women have our hearts broken, we're damned if we plot murder, and damned if we don't.

It's worth noting that, in love triangles, men come unhinged, too. But no one ever drags their professional life into the discussion. (If wife murderer Scott Peterson was accused of being an unfit pesticide salesman, I stand corrected.)

The hypocrisy points to an important question: How do we want our female leaders — passionate and unpredictable "like a woman," or controlled and calculated "like a man"?

Would we, deep down, really prefer that women stay home and stop meddling in areas that were once so neatly — so masculinely — defined? Or would we simply rather the nation's female role models abstain from the messy business of falling in love, so that we can forget they're sexual beings entirely?

Women are multi-faceted. I love that Nowak's NASA biography reports her hobbies as skeet shooting and growing African violets. I love how Clinton admits, in her autobiography, that her husband's infidelity left her "furious" and "gulping for air," but that she can still somehow manage to not assault Monica Lewinsky in a Florida parking garage.

Ultimately, a woman's going to pursue that which makes her happiest, and no amount of public scorn is going to stop her.

For what it's worth, though, I'd rather our next President approach life's challenges with a poker face than a pocket knife.

Innocence Glossed

SEX ED LANDS
CANDID MOM IN JAIL

I APOLOGIZE IN ADVANCE if my column ends abruptly today; chances are good I'll be hauled off to jail before I finish saying what I'm about to say.

You see, I did an unforgivable thing. Some might even call it abusive.

I allowed my fourth-grader to wander into the room while I was watching *Boston Legal*, during which two lawyers ravaged each other in office chairs, elevators and (heaven forgive them) a judge's chamber.

My son now has a twisted understanding of what it means to take the law into ones' own hands.

But it doesn't end there.

A few weeks ago, the boy saw his father and me making out in the kitchen while he was trying to eat his breakfast.

I didn't think much of his premature exposure to the tawdry under-belt of life until I heard that a Wisconsin mother was recently arrested — just want to make sure you read that right: a-r-r-e-s-t-e-d — for having a factual but explicit discussion about sex with her kids. Amy Smalley, 36, allegedly told her 11- and 15-year-old sons about some of her sexual experiences, described oral sex and showed them a vibrator.

Now, I'm not saying I want the woman baby-sitting my kids. Clearly there's a line between "educating" and "seriously grossing out," and she appears to have crossed it. The younger boy, not surprisingly, told a school counselor the discussion made him uncomfortable.

But felony? *Really?!*

Opponents of school-sponsored sex education are always saying the subject should be addressed at home, not in the classroom. But when a parent opens her mouth on the subject — as well as the, um, drawer on her night stand — she faces more than three years in prison and fines of up to $10,000.

All of which reminds me of a call I got recently from a parent at my son's school. It seems my 9-year-old had found a *Playboy* magazine sitting in plain view at the not-especially-kid-friendly home of a relative. Unbeknownst to me, he had perused the periodical (the "College Girls" issue, oy) and chosen to share his insights with his classmates the next day.

My husband and I talked with our son about age-appropriate reading material, and the downside of discussing girlie mags on the playground. But it didn't surprise me that he peeked at its pages; it's natural to be curious about anatomy and, well, dorm life.

No, what surprised me most was a comment this other parent made. "I'm sure you understand," he said, and he was very nice about the whole thing, but ... "We like to keep our kids innocent as long as we can."

We do?

The facts are these: Sex is as integral a part of human life as food, and sleep. And like rainwater rushing down a mountain, dodging rocks and circumnavigating trees to get to sea level, kids *will* learn about sex one way or another.

That's why I've always valued information over innocence, preparation over protection. So did Ms. Smalley, who, in the end, proved to be a protective mother after all. Still maintaining she did nothing wrong, she pled guilty and accepted a year of probation so her kids wouldn't have to stand trial against her — a far more traumatic experience than hearing about mom's adult-oriented romps.

She'll have to think twice now before answering her teens' questions about adulthood, which is sad. Until they come for me, I'm going to keep watching my sordid sitcoms and kissing my spouse willy-nilly. No pent-up lawmaker's going to tell me how to ...

You'll have to excuse me. Someone's pounding on my door.

Going Gay

WHY SHOULD PREACHERS HAVE ALL THE FUN?

I'M BORED TO TEARS with being straight.

It seems all the really cool people these days are gay: T.R. Knight from *Grey's Anatomy*. Sarah Paulson from *Studio 60 on the Sunset Strip*. Neil Patrick Harris from *How I Met Your Mother*.

From NBA player John Amaechi to 'N Sync heartthrob Lance Bass, it's in to be out. Being gay even made Mary Cheney and Candace Gingrich seem hip, for a few minutes.

The cultural cachet threatens to make anyone without a rainbow sticker on her bumper feel dreadfully dull. But there's hope for us hum-drum heteros.

Just look at Rev. Ted Haggard, big-time Bush supporter and founder of the New Life Church in Colorado Springs. In November, the evangelical preacher confessed to having paid a male hooker for sex over a period of three years — which was awkward, since he'd been publicly condemning homosexuality for years.

Miraculously, Pastor Ted recently announced that after just three weeks of intensive spiritual counseling, he has "discovered" that he is "completely heterosexual." Phew!

His swift return to righteousness didn't stop the married preacher from stepping down as his church's leader and announcing plans to flee, er, move to a new town. But perhaps that had less to do with his sexuality than with the methamphetamine he was fond of using during his frequent gay sex. No matter. The important thing is that the good reverend has settled on a sexuality that both he and the GOP can feel comfy with.

Gay conversion programs are nothing new. For years, Christian groups have been beseeching gays to fight their sinful urges and embrace the straight life. Focus on the Family, a religious nonprofit based in Haggard's hometown, helps men "overcome" homosexuality and "leave their gay identity behind" through prayer, counseling and — as best I can glean — male-bonding exercises.

Another group, Exodus International, promises liberation for those "looking for a way out" of same-sex attraction.

(This group also opposes laws that punish people who commit hate crimes against gays — which, I'm pretty sure, is not what Jesus would do.)

"You can lead a life of fulfillment and holiness as God intended," says the Exodus Web site, "a life far better than what you have experienced so far."

Damn if they don't make it sound nice ... and so simple!

So I decided to give it a try. If it's so easy to flip-flop one's fleshly fancies, why couldn't Exodus help me reverse my sexual identity? Why couldn't I use the same principles to go from garden variety man bait to rip-roaring lady lover?

I didn't expect it to be easy. Apart from a penchant for clunky shoes and occasional impure thoughts about Mariska Hargitay and Fergie (but not, like, at the same time or anything), I score fairly low on the lesbian scale.

But, hey, if those benevolent evangelicals could break a hypocrite like Haggard, surely they could help me.

I contacted all 11 of the group's California ministries and told them I was a straight mother of two hoping to "re-orient" with the Lord's guidance, lipstick aversion therapy, marathon viewings of *The L Word* or whatever it took.

"Can you advise me on how I might finally achieve what may very well be my destiny as a gay woman?" I asked. Their responses were disappointing, to say the least.

"Our ministry only helps people move towards a heterosexual identity," replied the director of one ministry. "We have not heard of any organizations that help people go the other way."

"This is not a change that I would recommend," explained another.

I'm not a person of faith, but I hold out hope that these groups will eventually see the value in, well, "going the other way." Heterosexuality is so 20th century and I'm guessing Haggard would be the first to admit that life without variety is its own sort of hell.

I look forward to the day when gay pop culture icons can team up with homophobic Bible thumpers for a fresh new take on conversion programs.

We could call it "Queer Eye for the Scared to Try."

Warning: Children in Charge

FOR PARENTS, there's nothing more gratifying than the white-hot itch of outrage. A hearty helping of peeved exasperation, coupled with a leisurely blame-laying session, can be such a delightful distraction from our own inequities as muddle-headed mothers and flawed fathers.

Kid Nation has been kind enough to provide our latest whipping post — but I'm not sure the ire is entirely deserved. The upcoming CBS reality show plunked 40 children in the middle of Pretty Much Nowhere, New Mexico, for 40 days with no contact with their parents. The kids' challenge: To turn an Old West-style movie set into a functioning society with a government, working store, hot meals, and someone to clean the outhouses.

Ranging in age from 8 to 15, the kids arrived on the set in April to less-than-cozy conditions: no electricity, bed rolls on the floor, extreme desert temperatures, and the only fresh water sloshing around in a well a quarter-mile from camp. The children each got $5,000 for taking part, and competed weekly for another $20,000. Anyone could opt to go home at any time, and a few did.

The show, which premieres this week, is understandably controversial. CBS was accused of skirting child labor laws, allowing them to work for 14-hour stretches. There were on-set injuries: a sprained arm, a burned face from cooking grease. Four of the children accidentally drank bleach from an unmarked bottle.

You can't blame critics for wagging their fingers at this exploitive enterprise. Face it: Network execs are callous ratings-grubbers who'd sell their own grannies into "reality" slavery *(So You Think You Can Knit; Pimp My Walker)* for a higher share of viewers.

And yes, any parent who'd sign a contract absolving the producers if their youngster should die or contract a sexually transmitted disease has clearly not been watching Lindsay, Britney, and Paris come of age: Does anyone really still think the spotlight is a great place for kids to grow up?

But I think there's another factor at play here, another secret sentiment driving our collective indignation over *Kid Nation*, which we've yet to even see: We're afraid these kids are gonna like it.

Admit it. We're all just a liiiiiittle bit worried that, given the chance to fly solo, these pre-teens are going to rise to the challenge and realize they can manage okay on their own. They can scramble eggs in a pinch. They can scrub latrines if need be. They don't technically need their parents; they may not even (gulp) miss them.

And then, by god, *what would we do?* If kids find out they're as smart, strong, and capable as us — and without our cynicism and increasing inability to recall the names of everyday nouns — the hierarchy of our households would topple!

Every "not until you've eaten your vegetables," every "not until you've finished your homework" would be met with a cheeky, "If I can haul well water, I can certainly manage my own fiber intake and study schedule. Jeez."

It says a lot that most *Kid Nation* kids — even the bleach-drinkers — chose to stay the whole 40 days despite tears, arguments, and an unpleasant little diva who snaps, "I'm a beauty queen. I don't do dishes!" But think about it. You were a kid once. What heat and hard labor would you have endured for the privilege of not being nagged about going outside in your clean socks? Or making your bed?

The *Kid Nation* trailer shows children shouting triumphantly as they thrust their filthy, candy-clutching fists toward the New Mexico sky. A voiceover says, "Can they succeed where adults have failed?" And the answer is, of course they can.

But for god's sake, *they* don't need to know that, do they?

Shaking My Faith in Quad

IN THE WEEKS before graduating UCLA, I made a pledge to myself: I would find a way back to college.

The route was inconsequential. Grad student. Janitor. The lady who licks envelopes in the chancellor's office. It didn't matter.

I didn't know what I wanted to do with my life, but I knew it would be more pleasant — easier, friendlier, prettier — if I did it on a campus.

College, for me, was a short-lived utopia. A quirky cultural convergence where the safety of childhood overlapped briefly, miraculously, with the freedom of adulthood.

Hemming the historic, litter-free quads of my alma mater was a sort of make-believe mini city with its own pizza parlor, bowling alley, library, post office and museum. It was an idyllic space, kind of like you picture Switzerland: everyone happy and good-looking with their health care paid for.

I had a university debit card that my parents loaded

up with cash for me to dispense on textbooks, nutritious lunches and the cappuccinos that fueled my all-nighters. I was playing grown-up, and the other 40,000 people on campus had agreed, quite sportingly, to play along.

To my glee, I was recently invited back on to a college campus to teach writing. Not much has changed in the hrmphzrmph years since I last lugged a backpack. College air is still more crisp — more buoyant with optimism, more lofty with intellect — than the stagnant and world-weary atmosphere hovering just outside its perimeter.

The promise of support is everywhere. Banners span each pristine walkway touting "Career Advancement!" "Transfer Achievement!" and "The Gateway to Success!" There are tutors and day care centers, scholarships and escorts to walk you to your car after dark.

Like parents helping a baby learn to walk, these programs exist solely to ensure that students, in the infancy of their maturity, never fall down.

I was sitting in my office hours last week, hoping some struggling student might seek my counsel, when I learned of the horrendous bloodshed at Virginia Tech. And I couldn't get the information to make sense. Not the stories, the photos, the on-the-scene videos. Not the quotes, the timelines, the memorials. Cognitively, I couldn't arrange them in a way that allowed me to believe the deadliest shooting in U.S. history had taken place at society's only remaining sanctuary for idealism.

It couldn't have. College is a haven. Somewhere to experiment with a safety net, to stumble but never fall. Not a place where a freshman and senior are gunned down in their dorms before breakfast.

It's a place to dream big and think carefully. To attend lectures in engineering buildings like Norris Hall and learn how to build. To make something out of nothing. To lay a steady and secure foundation, and reach ever upward from there.

Not a place of thoughtlessness. Of destruction. Of fear.

College is freedom: deciding whether to sleep in or haul ass to an 8 o'clock class; opting to party rather than study, and facing the consequences. It's not a campus-wide lockdown, an official notice to "stay away from all windows" or a madman chaining the exits to prevent your escape.

Students in French class don't flip their desks upside down for protection. Mechanics students needn't leap from second story windows. Those in computer class shouldn't team up to barricade doors that won't lock. (Why should they?) They don't hide in teacher's offices, or lay down on the floor beside bleeding bodies in the hopes of being mistaken for a corpse.

The ugly truth is that real life can be like that. Terrifying. Unpredictable. Unfair. Full of puncturing surprises and senseless loss.

But college isn't supposed to be.

The victims at Virginia Tech fell down. We let them fall. And in so doing, we watched a utopia topple.

Sinning Senators Are So Ho-Hum

GOOD GRIEF, it happened again: One of those awful press conferences at which a carefully dressed little man confesses to the world — while an explosion of flashbulbs reflects off his sweaty forehead — that his penis has been somewhere it probably ought not to have been.

Beside the elected statesman stands his humiliated wife, who has been coached by a callous crisis-management spinner to hold hands with her calamitously horny husband and radiate divine absolution. Because right now, she is the closest thing the American viewers have to God. And if she can forgive him, then so should we.

The latest lawmaker to step up to the "Forgive me, constituents, for I have sinned" podium is Louisiana Senator David Vitter. The Republican's phone number turned up on the client list of a Washington, D.C., escort service that federal prosecutors are calling a prostitution ring. He apologized and his wife, Wendy, who once told reporters she would go Lorena Bobbitt on her better half if he was ever caught cheating, assured us — with the most pained expression I've ever seen — their marriage was stronger than ever.

We may be seeing more of these episodes in the coming weeks if others of the escort service's 200,000 phone numbers are identified as legislators. What are the chances?

Commanders-in-Chief FDR and JFK had mistresses. Clinton had Monica. Los Angeles Mayor Antonio Villaraigosa just copped to a marriage-ending affair. And Vitter's Senate predecessor was Robert Livingston, who resigned when word got out that he was cheating on his wife.

Why do politicians have such trouble keeping their trousers zipped? Is it the stress of the job? The aphrodisiac of power? Are the women of Washington, D.C., really that much hotter than those in the rest of the world?

I've heard scientists speculate that men seek public office for the express, if not always conscious, purpose of gaining access to more sexual partners. ("It's just nature's way, darling. Don't be cross.") One thing's for sure: They have more energy than I do. I think about what it would take for a public person to carry on a secret affair (Disguises? Separate bank accounts? Dedicated cell phones?) and I'm exhausted before the fun part even begins. But the real question isn't why or how our officeholders cheat. It's whether their cheating makes them bad leaders.

I'm the last person you'd expect to forgive a philanderer;

I've seen too many people crushed by dalliances that probably felt harmless at the time. And as unlikely as I am to forgive a cheater, I'm even less likely to cut a Republican some slack. Especially a hypocritical one like Vitter who has been marching in the "family values" parade for years, and called the perennially canoodling Clinton "morally unfit to govern."

But, perhaps everyone's flawed in some way: an appetite for interns, an inflated ego, horrendous comic timing. And maybe our job as voters is to figure out how our politicians are flawed and either vote them the hell out of office or else shrug our shoulders and say, "Eh, I can live with that."

If we must continue to see these confessional press conferences, though, just once I'd like to see the mortified missus step up to the mike and say, "I'm divorcing this schmuck because he messed up our marriage. But I'm going to continue to vote for him, and you should, too, because he's good at his job. In fact, having humiliated me so thoroughly, he's bound to be an even better representative than he was before. Because I know from experience that after he's screwed someone, he's incapable of doing it again for a good, long time."

Here's the Buzz

MISSING BEES TURN UP CHEZ MOI

ON THE VERY SAME day that scientists announced that an alarming number of the country's honeybees had gone missing, I found them. Not the scientists; the bees. They were in my garage.

Experts converged on New York last week to discuss a disturbing national trend: the unexplained disappearance of tens of millions of bees, who have abandoned their hives never to return. The mystery, dubbed Colony Collapse Disorder, is being blamed on everything from genetically modified crops to the radiation from cell-phone towers. At worst, they said, it could result in ghastly food shortages since the insects' pollination helps produces a full third of our daily diet.

I can't pretend I'm a lover of bugs. Crawly, winged, "beneficial" or otherwise, I'd just as soon squash them as look at them. Even ladybugs and butterflies trigger my gag reflex. So it is with some pride that I confess my evolution — throughout the years — from a screamer who would flee the house with arms flailing at the sight of a mosquito, to a cold-blooded sniper who can flatten a fly with a magazine or crush a spider in a Kleenex without so much as a break in my conversation.

But this was different.

My son was shooting hoops in the driveway when he heard the buzzing. A swarm of bees was hovering near the corner of the garage. The next day, an exterminator — whose motto is "Bees are our bees-ness" — revealed these droning, ominous pests had found a hole in our eaves, infiltrated our exterior wall, and built a sort of high-rise luxury estate in there.

Floor to ceiling, the wall was thick with solid honeycomb. These bees had been busy for six months. While we were sitting down to Thanksgiving dinner, they were nearby, extruding wax from their abdomens. As we were leaving cookies for Santa, they were chewing the wax to make it malleable. When we were exchanging Valentine's Day cards, they were shaping the wax into intricate, hexagonal little apartments to house their honey, pollen, and larvae. Enterprising little bastards.

Our expert guessed there were ten-freaking-thousand bees in our wall — and advised we destroy them. Left alone, they might find their way inside our house in large numbers. Their honey would leak through our walls and attract ants, wasps, and rats, and if you think I'm squeamish about bugs, you ought to see me face-to-face with a rodent.

We were told there was no way to remove the bees without killing them, and to be honest, I didn't give it a second thought. Eight hundred dollars later, the walls were flushed with poison and the workers set about digging out the once golden, gleaming honeycomb — now a dry, white bee graveyard.

Dead bees littered my driveway. And though the sight of a lifeless insect used to bring me some measure of peace, I was surprised at my remorse. It's not that they were cute: They're fuzzy and oddly jointed, with random black threads protruding from their crooked little carcasses. But they had been so ... productive. And highly motivated. And scarce, for god's sake.

What beeswax is it of mine if nature's hardest workers — the very creatures that bring us watermelons, pumpkins, berries, and almonds — want to play house behind my drywall?

I had some Poe-like moments when I kept hearing buzzing in my kitchen. In my hair. I found one dead on the floor of my car and when I tried to fling it out the window, it bounced off the door and came hurtling back at me.

Our bee guy told us the bee shortage is worse in the eastern states; honeybees, so far, are still showing up for work in California's fields. His words couldn't wash the bee blood from my hands. But it did take some of the sting out of it.

Church and State Collide on Highway

THIS JUST IN: Rational thought is backed up for miles along South Carolina's roadways, where a serious traffic collision between Church and State has left our Constitution in critical condition.

And it's left Atheists a little cross.

The state recently approved a series of government-issued license plates bearing the words "I BELIEVE" and the image of a Christian cross in front of a stained-glass window. In addition to boasting their state-sanctioned love for square dancing, wild turkeys, and Dale Earnhardt Jr., South Carolina residents can now share their devotion to Jesus Christ with anyone lucky enough to be eating their dust.

The plate was proposed by Republican state Senator Larry Grooms "to allow people of faith to have an expression of their belief." Apparently ichthys fish and "God is my copilot" bumper stickers just weren't converting heathens like they used to.

An identical license plate was considered and rejected in Florida in April. Even South Carolina's Governor Mark Sanford, a Christian himself, declined to sign the bill, arguing, "The largest proclamation of one's faith ought to be in how one lives one's life."

It seems the governor lives his own life by inaction: He refused to outright veto the bill. Which means the following conversation will soon be taking place on a Beaufort boulevard:

"Did you get the license number of the guy who mowed you down, ma'am?"

"No, officer. But I can tell you this: He believes."

Secular outrage aside, I find the plates curious. Leaping onto Chevy tails along with South Carolina's Shriners, Amateur Radio Club, and Omega Psi Phi fraternity makes Christianity seem less like a personal spiritual understanding and more like a weekend hobby. And not a cool one.

More to the point: If your faith is so strong that it would inspire you to voluntarily stand in line at the DMV — and let's face it, that's strong — then why do you need it stamped in cold, hard metal on your vehicle's ass?

Practically speaking, I see the plates as a handy visual warning to other motorists that the driver in front of them may be logic-challenged. But there are greater issues at risk here.

Critics, including the ACLU, say the state-issued plates are a government endorsement of religion. South Carolina's DMV doesn't offer tags emblazoned with a Star of David, a Buddha, or even a pentagram. It doesn't sell an "IT'S ALL HOOEY" plate with an evolving Darwin fish on it. And whereas motorists pay up to $70 for other specialty plates, "I BELIEVE" is offered — miracle of miracles — for fewer than six bucks.

We all know Christianity is our nation's unofficial religion the way English is our unofficial language, — i.e., there's nothing unofficial about it. But what about when the state endorses one political ideology over another? Those of us who worship at the Church of Reason, whose greatest faith is in Democracy, may consider that a far greater sin.

In May, South Carolina (a.k.a. the Palmetto State) approved specialty plates whose sale benefits 22 abortion-alternative health clinics across the state. The plates read, "Choose Life," with the "I" formed by a pretty palmetto tree — the symbol on the state's flag and seal.

"Choose Life" plates are currently available in more than a dozen states. California's not one of them. But as long as we're imprinting religious and political ideology onto government equipment, I saw a bumper sticker once that would make an excellent Golden State plate: "May the fetus you save be a black, gay, Wiccan Democrat."

Mommy's a Liar

SOMETIMES THE TRUTH is gross.
 I know this because I hail from the too-much-information school of parenting. I can't help it. As a reporter and a storyteller, I see every innocent question as an opportunity to further the wide-eyed wonderer's understanding of this wacky world.

But my bent toward full disclosure often backfires, leaving my kids slightly confused and thoroughly disgusted: "Jeez, Mom, I just asked what a wart is. Did we really have to talk about genital disease?"

Still, I'd rather err on the side of unflinching truth than have my kids thinking that I hide facts from them, or worse, that I outright lie. Honesty is the holy grail in our household, the highest of all virtues, the one safeguard that will keep you out of trouble even when all your other behavior — greed, spite, laziness — has been seriously uncool.

But not all families share that value, as a Dallas mother proved recently. The woman helped her 6-year-old daughter write the winning essay in a contest for Hannah Montana concert tickets. The essay explained how the girl's father, a sergeant in Iraq, was killed by a roadside bomb. Contest judges awarded her four tickets, airfare, accommodations and a makeover — which is really the very least you could do for a girl who lost her daddy to a senseless, and ceaseless, war.

The problem, though, is that she actually didn't. The father is alive and living in Texas. He's not a soldier. Never was. When confronted with the truth, the girl's mother explained that "we did whatever we could do to win." (Hey, at least she's honest.) The prize was rescinded and awarded to another contestant whose mother, presumably, was not a devious cheat.

I suppose there's a place in every family for lies — only let's not call them "untruths" or "fibs," shall we? If you can agree that lies are lies, I can agree that they're sometimes useful. I'm actually a proponent of the Lie-to-Spare-Someone's-Feelings, for instance. No one ever died from a well-placed "Wow, thanks, Aunt Ann, it's ... really ... something!"

I've been known, too, to partake of the Lie-By-Omission (i.e., not telling your toddler that the dreaded baby-sitter is coming because, um, he didn't ask) and the Lie-For-Your-Own-Good (i.e., "Unfortunately, we're all out of Doritos. Would you like some wheat toast instead?")

Sometimes we lie to young children to help them fit a new fact into their narrow system of categorization. Calling a bran muffin a cupcake, for example, simply means "It's neither cheese nor vegetables. You should eat it." And calling a tampon a Band-Aid is just our way of saying "Don't worry about it. It has good reason to be in my purse."

Ask parents and they'll tell you the hardest question to answer honestly is this one: "Is it going to hurt?" But I think our real moment of truth comes when our kids catch us lying to others: sneaking sodas into a movie theater in our purse, telling a telemarketer that we're in the middle of dinner.

I remember once hearing my dad tell his boss that he couldn't come to work because his father-in-law had died. And while it was true, it had happened three years earlier — and my dad hadn't cared much for the guy even then.

But if lying in front of your children is bad, then *helping* your children lie — and doing it not to, like, fight global warming, but for seats at a cheesy Disney pop concert — is worse.

When my son saw the headline "Mother Lied to Win Hannah Montana Contest," he asked me about it and I told him — every ugly detail, as is my habit. But I was heartened to discover, in his reaction, that parents' calculated lies can be even more disgusting than our uncensored truths.

"Wow," he said. "That's kind of sick."

A Formula for Guilt

TAINTED BABY FOOD LEAVES KIDS ILL, PARENTS REMORSEFUL

IT'S EASY TO BECOME desensitized to newspaper photos. Hurricanes. Train wrecks. Kidnappings. As we flip blithely through oversized, peril-heralding pages, the images become small, muddy-colored windows into worlds we can't really relate to, and don't especially want to visit.

Every once in a while, though, an image still tweaks me right where it counts. Like the recent photo of a frowning Chinese infant strapped to a hospital bed, his wrists restrained to keep him from pulling out the various needles and tubes taped to his bare chest and arms.

He's one of more than 50,000 babies who've been sickened by industrially tainted infant formula in China. And his picture hit me hard: I had chills, then nausea, then tears. I had empathy, then anger … and then guilt.

Which is strange, because researchers confirmed it wasn't me who killed four babies and left 13,000 hospitalized. It was melamine, a white, fire-resistant powder used to make plastic. When added to watered-down formula, it makes the product appear higher in protein. When ingested, it can cause kidney stones and renal failure.

The Chinese government has arrested more than a dozen melamine suppliers and contaminated milk manufacturers. But that doesn't dull the agony the babies, and their parents, are enduring.

"When I look into his eyes, I feel so guilty," Mo Chongjian told the *L.A. Times* after learning that his year-old son has stones in both kidneys. "I couldn't protect him."

I can't say I know what it feels like to stand in line at a public hospital with your wailing infant, waiting for the ultrasound that will tell you whether his food source has poisoned him. But I know what it doesn't feel like. It doesn't feel like you're a good parent.

My sons consumed a lot of formula because I had trouble nursing them. For whatever reason, I couldn't produce enough breast milk to keep them satisfied, or even healthy. I knew from childbirth classes and parenting books that, nutritionally, breast-feeding is the best thing a mother can do for her kids. Studies show children who nurse are somehow smarter. Plus breast milk is free and — unlike formula — doesn't stain. Fantastic!

No sooner was my son delivered from my womb than he was lifted to my breast for his first gulps of sustenance. Providing this customized baby fuel known as "liquid gold" was my first job as a new mother, and I wanted so desperately to rise to the role and prove my maternal mettle.

But I couldn't. No amount of pumping, herbal

supplementing, or even beer-chugging (a nurse told me secretly that the yeast might help) could encourage my feeble postpartum physique to step up production on the newborn nectar.

I hired consultants. I filled prescriptions. I put myself and my firstborn through too many sweaty sob sessions trying to convince us both that failure wasn't an option. But ultimately, he drank formula. Gulped it. Guzzled it. Chugged it down with a glee, and an expression of utter peace, that I had never seen cross his face before. And despite my malfunctioning mammaries, he thrived.

Photos from China's formula fiasco brought back the feelings of desperation, failure and, as Mr. Chongjian said, the guilt that marked my first few months of motherhood.

What I've learned since then is this: You get thousands of opportunities to prove your parental pluck, to protect and provide for your children. The parents of China's ailing infants may find, as I did, that parental success isn't measured in how well we control the uncontrollable. It's in how we react to those events, getting our kids whatever they need — be it food or medicine — to find peace.

Here's hoping they get that chance.

Another Sticky Mess for O.J.

THE JUICE IS UNDER THE GAVEL AGAIN

SURELY BY NOW O.J. Simpson has spent more time in courtrooms than he ever did on gridirons. The Juice is under the gavel again, standing trial for kidnapping and (yawn) armed robbery. Prosecutors say he led gunmen into a Vegas hotel room last year to rob a sports memorabilia dealer. The defense insists the former NFL running back was just trying to retrieve stuff that belonged to him, including photos of his children. Those would be the kids who were asleep inside their mother's Brentwood condominium in 1994 while she and a friend were being stabbed to death just outside. Acquitted of the gruesome murders in a criminal trial, but found liable for the deaths in a civil trial, Simpson swore he'd spend the rest of his life hunting down the "real" killer of Nicole Brown Simpson and her friend Ron Goldman.

For a while, O.J. appeared to be scouring the world's finest golf courses in search of the outlaw. Then last year he wrote the cheeky tell-all *If I Did It*, explaining how he would have slaughtered his ex-wife, if he were the type of guy to do that sort of thing. A judge awarded book rights to Goldman's family as restitution, and the stomach-turning tome has sold more than 100,000 copies.

From the beginning, the story of O.J.'s dive from celebrated football great to despised prison evader has been marked by mind-boggling idiocy. Not only his — but my own.

I was a young reporter working at the *Brentwood News* when word of the double homicide spread through the tiny Los Angeles suburb. My editor sent me to Nicole's condo for some on-the-scene reporting, and the news was so fresh that I found myself alone there.

Police tape was strewn around the Bundy Drive lawn where the victims had fallen. Their bodies were gone, but patches of dark, sticky blood still marked the walkway. I was too green — both inexperienced and, now, queasy — to translate these disturbing observations into a compelling or meaningful story. I stood stupidly with my blank notepad, staring at the gooey and irrefutable evidence of the previous night's violence ... and wondering why I hadn't gotten a job at some cushy advertising firm like the rest of my friends.

By the next day, of course, the surrounding sidewalks were shoulder-to-shoulder with international news crews and rubber-necking L.A. residents. You couldn't get within 50 feet of the crime scene, but my editor (whose staffing instincts clearly needed sharpening) sent me back to cover the "media frenzy." I was parking my car when a misinformed radio announcer shrieked, "They're taking a body out of the house right now!" I flung off my platform shoes and began sprinting toward the action, only to trip on the hem of my palazzo pants (hey, it was 1994) and slide face-down across the asphalt, tearing my clothes. Bleeding and barefoot, I hobbled toward the crowd with my camera aimed at the throngs of sweaty thrill-seekers who had swarmed the once quiet neighborhood.

I didn't get any photos. Because it turned out I hadn't brought any film. In fact, the best scoop I got all day was a dip into the office freezer, grabbing ice for my throbbing knee. But I did wind up on the cover of the *L.A. Times* the next day. Their photographer, equipped with film, snapped a terrific crowd shot with a wounded cub reporter in the center, looking bewildered. Bungling that assignment is one of my greatest professional regrets. I missed the story of a lifetime. Twice.

But regret is what makes us better. I'm smarter now. More experienced. Less intimidated by things I don't immediately understand. And I'm not afraid to ask questions. Like this one: Why hasn't regret taught O.J. a damn thing?

The Swing of Things

PLAYGROUNDS LOOK LIKE such innocent places. Coated in primary colors and plopped atop shock-absorbent tanbark, park equipment has no sharp edges, no pokey corners. What could be more liberating?

But anyone who's logged pre-nap hours there will tell you the freedom is pure illusion.

Like life, playgrounds are governed by rigid, unwritten rules that can puzzle and plague you until you learn how to work within them.

Or around them.

Upon entering a playground, for example, you're expected to smile at other mothers even if they don't look like people you could possibly be friends with. Though you never officially signed up, you are now part of a club: the Desperate to Get My Toddler Out of My House Club. By not acknowledging other members of said club with a "Hi, how'd we get *here?*" sort of nod, you appear to be "too cool" for the club, which is not OK. The other moms will say rude things about your rump when you're bending over to retrieve a sippy cup from the sand, and who wants that, really?

While friendliness among females is encouraged, speaking to other womens' husbands — even just to say "Has your kid rented that swing for the day or can we get a turn?" — is strictly verboten and will only inspire more butt mockery. Don't grin at other daddies, especially the ones wearing "I Heart Hot Moms" T-shirts. And under no circumstances should you offer to be the "teeter" to a hunky dad's "totter," no matter how pathetic and lonely he looks sitting on the thing by himself.

If, in an effort to instill your child with respect for social rules and public safety, you insist that he slide *down* the slide rather that climb up it, you'll be labeled a micromanaging spirit-quasher.

If, in an attempt to encourage his creativity and curiosity, you allow him to climb up the slide, be prepared for your new reputation as a reckless scofflaw. (Also, have an ice pack handy for when his creative and curious teeth meet with the fast-moving feet of a child who comes bounding *down* the slide, the way God intended. And yes, you can tell which side of this argument I come down upon.)

Playground protocol is complex, as evidenced by the rarely verbalized but strictly observed Sharing Treaty: A parent is never (ever!) to offer another child a snack of any kind. Not a pretzel, a Goldfish cracker or a single red grape. There are allergy issues. Ingredient anxieties. And the ugly implication that the child isn't being properly fed by her own mother.

Likewise will that mother blush and apologize if her daughter asks another mom to hand over a single Cheerio, even if she does it politely.

Whereas snacks are considered oddly personal, though, toys are treated as communal property the second they hit the sandbox. When another kid outrageously rips a truck, trike, ball or bat from your child's hands, you must demand that your child "share," which, in park lingo, means, "Let it go. We'll snatch it back later when he's not looking."

Real life is not like this, of course. As grown-ups, we are not required to share our cars with strangers who admire them in the parking lot. We are not obliged to pluck out our iPod ear buds and hand them over to weirdos at the gym who say "gimme."

But the playground is different. On the planet of parenthood, it's like its own sovereign nation with strange and stringent customs that feel as foreign to us as ... well, as trying to scurry up a slippery slide. Don't be fooled by the cushy padding underfoot. Bungle your jungle gym etiquette, mama, and you'll land with a painful thud.

I Killed the Tooth Fairy

SORRY

AFTER A DISTINGUISHED CAREER of doling out quarters in exchange for incisors, the Tooth Fairy died Monday — on my bedspread, amid a sprinkling of premolars, hand-written notes, and a bottle of common craft store glitter.

Born of a child's yen for magic and a parent's gift for deception, the centuries-old Ms. Fairy was useful in soothing children's understandable anxiety over losing small but significant body parts to the stubborn stick of a Starburst or the brutish yank of a string tied to a doorknob. You'd think the idea of a wily nymph infiltrating their bedrooms to retrieve dental detritus while they sleep would freak out most kids. But, in fact, her legend brought comfort to untold ragamuffins, inexplicably but effectively distracting them from even the gaping, fleshy hole now lurking in their once-craggy gums.

But earlier this week — in a moment as sudden and startling as the one that separates a "loose tooth" from a "lost tooth" — the fairy perished.

And I'm the one who killed her. Although, to be fair, my 9-year-old had already maimed her; I was just putting her out of her misery.

After more than a dozen personal rounds of the universal tooth-loss cycle (wiggle-yank-pillow-cash, wiggle-yank-pillow-cash), my son's preadolescent skepticism finally got the better of his juvenile faith. And while we all know human disease begins with medical symptoms — a nagging cough, a sharp pain — I've learned the demise of mythic figures begins with questions.

Ghastly, gut-wrenching, and altogether quite rational questions.

"Mom, how come when you lose a tooth on vacation, the Tooth Fairy doesn't leave purple fairy dust on your pillow?"

Well...

"Why do you still get money when you accidentally spit your tooth down the sink drain and can't leave it for her?"

Um...

"The note she left last time was burnt around the edges like a cool old pirate map, and this one is straight and plain and boring. Do you think she's mad at me?"

Yes. Probably.

When the Toothless Interrogator went to bed last week after sacrificing a beloved bicuspid to a stale Tootsie Roll, he left a note for the fairy reading, "Cash please. As much as you can." When he awoke the next morning and accused the poor slandered pixie of not only being cheap but of stealing a gold coin from his piggy bank and trying to pass it off as a new one (for the record, I assure you, she did not), I knew a mercy killing was the only way to preserve her dignity.

I quietly took the fourth-grade cynic into my room, sat him down gently on my bed, and pulled a secret box from the back of a dresser drawer. I opened it and laid all its evidence in front of him — evidence of my love, evidence of my lies. Thirteen polished white pebbles clicked and clacked as they spilled out before him. Old notes scrawled in silver cursive rustled as I unfurled them. And the plastic jar of, ahem, fairy dust hit the blanket with a graceless thud.

We stared at it all, together, in silence. His eyes welled up a bit, and he pouted for several minutes, refusing to speak to me while sorting his resentment from his embarrassment from his disappointment.

It's never easy burying a friend, but his grief was ultimately soothed by the promise of the future — a time when he would get to help us perpetrate the same ruthless deception on his poor, naïve little brother, who still has a mouthful of baby teeth.

In his own way, then, he has pledged to see Ms. Fairy's death avenged. An eye for an eye, as they say...

Mom Envy

TENSION'S TIGHT BETWIXT WORKING AND STAY-AT-HOME MOMS

YOU OVER THERE. That's right, you in the velour hoodie with the Venti Macchiato. I have to talk to you.

And you, too: The one dashing off to your car as fast as your pressed pencil skirt will let you run. Slow down for a second. You need to hear this.

It's drop-off time at school and, like most mornings, little circles of stay-at-home moms are pooling by the gate, near the office, in the parking lot. In pony-tails and baseball caps, they make playdates, share stories about head lice and commiserate over soccer schedules.

A working mom skitters past in a tailored suit and gleaming pumps. She's late for a meeting, but dials up a smile for the chatter-clatch moms, who wave at her. One of them — a petite brunette with no make-up and a dollop of crusted oatmeal on her yoga top — hollers over her shoulder in a tone that wasn't intended to sound bitchy: "Wow. Don't you look nice."

But between those five seemingly innocuous words lies the ugly tension that exists between moms who punch a timecard and moms who don't. And it's really rather stupid.

God bless feminism, but an abundance of life choices can make a gal paranoid. Those who choose Plain Ol' Mom as an occupation assume our suited sisters will secretly chide us for abandoning our professional potential. Those who opt for a paycheck figure our home-maker counterparts will tisk-tisk us for being selfish, or missing out on our kids' childhoods.

But it's not true and I'll tell you why.

A former desk jockey myself, I recently gave up the monotony of memos and mailrooms for the privilege of working at home. And while I still have deadlines, I'm able to linger longer at drop-off — abandoning my identity as a Mom With an Outrageous Dry Cleaning Bill and joining the ranks of the Moms Who Have Time to Schmooze.

What I didn't realize before I'd been on both sides is that it's not judgment that flows between the two camps. It's jealousy.

And, OK, a little bit of resentment. The mom who works all day has to choose, some mornings, between curling her hair and fixing her kids' lunches. She lost the opportunity to stop at Starbucks when she had to spend six minutes removing dog hair from her trousers with duct tape.

So after shoving her child out of the car with a half-hearted "Have fun at after-school care!" she can't fathom how the latte-wielding sweat suit set gets to stand around dishing dirt about the principal — she wants to dish dirt! and comparing gyms — she wants to belong to a gym! — when she has to be downtown for a conference call in exactly ... damn, three minutes ago.

Meanwhile, the ladies of leisure see in the blur of rayon running past them a symbol of grown-up life. They envy corporate moms for having a reason to dress up, an excuse to wear perfume and a watch. Just once they'd like to skip Pilates and go hang out in an office where people bring donuts for no reason. They wonder how their life might feel different if they were not the default chaperone for all second-grade field trips. If they were faced with interesting problems that couldn't be solved with a cookie, an ice pack or a time out.

But what if, instead of envying one another's choices, we supported them? Listen up, Leisure Mom: Tomorrow, raise your coffee in a toast to your amiga-in-pantyhose as she passes, and say "Go get 'em, Gorgeous!" Workaday Mom, be sure to shout back a genuine "Thanks for chaperoning the field trip today!" and invite your unhurried comrade to gossip with you over lunch.

Even better: Tell her she'll need to dress up.

Hang the Potty

BLOWING THE LID OFF TOILET TRAINING

THERE ARE CERTAIN MILESTONES a parent savors. First words. First steps. First day of school. But others, honestly, are more hassle than hooray. Potty training is one of those.

This is not a popular thing to say out loud. Magazines, preschool teachers and child-development experts tell us, in strange and stilted language, that supporting our children's natural inclination toward independent toileting is one of the greatest gifts we can give them blah blah blah. They insist our toddlers' ability to conquer the commode is tied to self-esteem, cognitive development and probably (I stopped reading after that) their future earning potential and ability to please a woman.

At least that's what Freud would say.

But you can flush all that right down the bowl, as far as I'm concerned. I'm washing my hands of potty training. My 2-year-old is already an accomplished human being. He can pour his own drink and fix himself a snack. He can fetch a hammer for his dad. He can even put on his own socks, which is no easy task when you consider the number of wayward toes one must wrangle into that tiny elasticized hole.

But he has no desire whatsoever to, er, take command of the throne. The kid's rapturously happy in Huggies and I've decided to let him stay that way. Forever.

Since experts warn that potty-pushing can lead to emotional and health problems, and since Pull-Ups and Depend undergarments can carry my son well into maturity, why not skip the loo entirely?

Don't get me wrong. I don't love diapering and would gladly give up the effort, expense and environmental guilt the chore demands: the mess-cleaning, ointment spreading and hand-washing, the frequent trips out to the trash, the alarming sound of my own voice bellowing "GET your hands out of there!"

But at least that's a chaos I'm used to. It's a familiar mayhem. Whereas a tot in underpants presents all sorts of fresh and frightening but equally icky problems.

I've been through potty training before, with my older child. I trained hard for the race to get my firstborn out of diapers, printing reward charts, shelling out for musical potty seats and Wiggles step stools, speaking of underwear in reverent tones, as though it were the pinnacle of human innovation. I had a video on endless loop in the living room that warbled a demonic song called "Super Duper Pooper."

And all for what?

So I could slam on my brakes on the freeway, pull off into the emergency lane and release the boy from his car seat with one hand while frantically fitting a gallon-sized Ziplock bag onto a portable potty seat with the other each time my briefs-sporting spawn felt the urge to wail "I need to go potty!"

Potty training may "free" a family from diapers, but it also shackles them to public restrooms, where sophisticated, self-aware, independent toileters take horrific glee in running their hands along the walls, dropping their toys into the john and sliding back and forth under stall doors to say "hi" to all the nice ladies.

It's an experience I'm not eager to repeat. And so, though I realize it will be awkward for him at sleep-over camp and, well, on the high-school swim team, my youngest child is welcome to wrap his rump in Pampers for as long as he likes.

And if the experts chide me for depriving him of a crucial, character-building life skill, I'll tell them to blame it on my desperate, irrepressible, long-developing urge for order. Maybe I'm anal retentive.

At least that's what Freud would say.

Thank You, Officer. No, Really.

I KNEW IT BEFORE his hulking, uniformed frame filled my passenger-side window. I knew it even before his patrol car crept quietly up behind me, centering itself in my rear-view mirror.

I had been speeding.

He clocked me at 80 mph in a 65 zone, but I was doing 90 before his radar locked onto my hastening Honda. I was late to fetch my son from preschool. Rather, I was about to be late, because late is not something I allow myself to be. I had left work in plenty of time but then, calculating an extravagant surplus of eight minutes, decided to first stop and pick up a prescription my other son needed. The errand took longer than I had hoped, and my cunning plan was to compensate for the tactical error by endangering countless lives on the highway.

God forbid my 2-year-old should have to ask, "Where's my mommy?"

There's that highly charged 30-second window between

the moment your tires come to rest on the road's shoulder and the moment the officer says, "Do you know why I pulled you over?" Options ricochet through your racing mind: How do you play this? Outright denial? Feigned ignorance? Unabashed groveling?

For the first time in my life, I chose contrition, straight-up. Even as I sat there, hands on the wheel at 10 and 2, humiliated by the "gotcha" grins of passing motorists, I knew I had earned the ticket and every inconvenience — fines, court appearances, traffic court — that it would cost me.

I deserved it. I was humbled by it. And despite what I may have involuntarily muttered about the cop's manhood as I slowed my time-traveling torpedo to a schedule-stymieing, efficiency-impeding halt, I was actually (oh, it hurts to even type it) grateful for it.

Because the ticket I drove away with is more than a hastily scrawled traffic citation. It's a bright yellow metaphor — and much-needed wake-up call — for the reckless pace of my life.

I could blame it on Santa Barbara's high cost of living. Or my decision to work full time while raising kids. Or the flawed personality of an over-achiever.

But the truth is we all struggle with work-life balance these days. We all neglect our health to nurture our careers, and slight our friendships to make time for our families. We all act as though a minute not spent in pursuit of income, or in completion of household chores, is a minute squandered.

As busy and goal-oriented as we are, though, we can be

shockingly lazy about our vices. We engage in foolhardy behaviors that help us through the day — chugging wine or mainlining coffee, scarfing donut holes, tearing through speed limits — figuring we'll hit the brakes as soon as it gets "dangerous."

When I was pulled over by the Highway Patrolman (whose name, according to his expeditious handwriting, is Officer MTcliH), my operating principle was productivity at all costs — and I'm lucky the natural consequence of my folly was a slap on the wrist rather than a body-mangling wreck.

I was late to pick up my kid from school that day, but I didn't rush through the afternoon the way I normally would. In fact, something odd happened. Rather than checking email while my kids watched TV, or folding laundry while they did their chores, we actually played together. Finding ourselves plopped on the driveway beside a bucket of sidewalk chalk, we colored and scribbled all over the tires of my car. Tires that had earlier been pushed to their performance limit now sat idle, their only function to foster our amusement. Our togetherness.

I still find myself speeding some days, and trying to squeeze too many half-assed accomplishments into too few minutes. But I don't want to spend every waking minute in the fast lane. There's a freedom, really, in acknowledging life's limits, speed and otherwise. I'm no expert at it yet, but I'll get there eventually.

Better late than never.

You Camp Be Serious

AS MUCH AS I HATE to see it go, it's good summer's nearing a close.

Parents (or at least this parent) get sloppy when school's out and the strict wake, work, wake, work routine of the school year melts into an amorphous, three-month spree of float, eat, nap ...

I'm embarrassed at how easily the rules I set up with my children's best interest in mind — dietary guidelines, hygiene habits — are overturned by the warbling notes of a passing ice cream truck and the compelling swimming-pool-as-bathtub argument.

The justification for such anarchy, of course, is that it's only temporary. We know that a few months of slippery discipline between the end-of-school potluck and the back-to-school potluck won't kill a kid.

Where our logic goes wrong, though — where our laissez-faire parenting practices may have disastrous long-term effects — is in our funding of frivolous summer camps.

Surf Camp. Archery Camp. Circus Camp, for god's sake.

In my rush to secure some blissful alone time — time to write without fielding the dreaded, "Mom, I'm bored, bored, BORED!" refrain — I signed my 8-year-old up for every camp he showed interest in. Broadway musical camp? Sure. Dog obedience camp? OK. Jedi Camp (where *Star Wars*-obsessed adults educate giddy little boys in the ways of The Force)? Um, alright. Truth is, they sounded fun even to me; and the more fun they were, the more likely I'd get some peace and quiet to do my work.

But as summer tapers off like the point of a snow cone, and I reflect on the $1,000 I've just invested in my son's development as a human being, I'm a little concerned. Because what I now have is not a fourth-grader who's appreciative of R&R and eager to return to academics with a clear head.

What I have is a kid torn between a career as an actor and a puppy trainer — who now thinks it's OK for grown men to wear Jedi robes and carry light sabers in public.

My girlfriend sent her son to rock guitar camp — which culminated in a deafening performance of Black Sabbath's "Iron Man," during which her boy wore spiked hair, an Ozzy grimace, and a worrisome twinkle in his eye.

"When we enroll our children in these camps," she now wonders, "what are we encouraging them to do, really? Are we aware they may actually find their niche? And we may inadvertently be signing up for years of metal rock concerts?"

According to the American Camp Association, there

are more than 12,000 camps operating this summer, and most are aimed at thrilling kids: Hollywood Stuntman Camp. Fashion Camp? *Gold-Panning?!* But plenty are designed to please parents.

And wouldn't our camp fees be better spent at, say, Healthspace Cleveland's Pre-Med Camp, where kids "explore career opportunities in health care" while donning scrubs and dissecting organs. In the photo, they look like kidneys, but I wouldn't know, as I spent my summers, (ahem) weaving lanyards.

How about San Jose's Web Architects Camp, where pre-teens design and publish an Internet site for the company of their dreams? Or Global Youth Village in Bedford, Virginia, where teens learn time management, goal setting, and resume writing? (Did I mention my son is now skilled in dog poop disposal? I wonder if there's money in that.)

I have a friend who flew her 11-year-old to the Midwest this summer for two whole weeks of intensive Japanese language camp; the tongue of our future world leaders.

Now that's a smart mom — a year-round parent whose diligence doesn't melt in the heat of summer. Because if you think about it, she didn't just get more peace of mind then I did; she got more peace and quiet.

Once Upon a Cool Mom

I THOUGHT I WAS going to be the cool mom. The fun one. The one whose house all the kids wanted to come play at because I let them drink soda and say "butt-head" while we all played *Star Wars* Monopoly inside a hastily engineered living-room pillow fort.

Like pillow forts, such fantasies prove easily toppled.

Still, it came as quite a shock recently when I overheard my 9-year-old describing me to a school buddy.

They were disappointed because I refused to pay them a fat dollar to buy lemonade they had made from the lemons in my backyard, and were serving in my paper cups, while I cleaned up their mess in the kitchen. It seemed to me a fair lesson in economics and the distribution of labor. But the fourth-graders didn't see it that way.

"I know," said my exasperated son to his glum chum. "But she's not ... like ... totally evil."

Perhaps I should be happy, since the statement was clearly made in my defense.

But: *evil?*

I'm the mom who livened up trips to the post office with a Silly Walk Contest. The one who dragged the boy out into thunderstorms to splash in mud puddles as we squealed from the cold. The one who taught him to belch, for chrissake.

And it grieves me that I don't know how I went from the Fun Mom to the Shower Enforcer. The Homework Reminder. The Cookie Monitor.

When did I become She Who Will Not Play Along?

I admit that as I age, I'm less and less willing to bend down and pick up Legos, or flop around on the trampoline, or make a lunch of chili cheese fries. But if age were the only factor, I wouldn't see my parents — people I recall growing more peevish and despotic as my adolescence approached — now serving my kids cupcakes for dinner, letting them stay up past *Conan* and encouraging the sort of sponge-defying messes that make me grind my teeth.

If I may shirk some of the blame, perhaps a parent's fun-factor naturally — and necessarily — shrinks as her children grow.

When it occurs to her that these small people are not merely her adorable little pals — and that despite their inability to say the letter R or master effective nose-blowing techniques — they will eventually become independent adults, then the task of ensuring their happiness changes dramatically. It no longer means simply making them smile. It means increasing the odds that they'll be healthy (i.e., can swallow a steamed vegetable without gagging). And successful (i.e., can multiply eight by six in under three minutes). And loved (i.e., can recall with some certainty the last time they bathed).

Which really sucks the fun out of being a parent, if you ask me. Because my son and his buddies aren't the only ones who cringe when they hear un-fun phrases coming out of my mouth, ghastly rebukes like, "I'm just disappointed in you, that's all" and "I don't care for the tone in your voice, young man."

I hate it, too.

But I'm optimistic that a time will come when my kid and I can be play pals again. Perhaps it won't be until he has children, and I can invite them over to drink soda and say "butt-head" inside a precarious pillow fort — and then send them home for their own parents to fret over. Maybe then I'll be lauded as the cool grandma, or even Nana Banana, the funnest old lady that ever bankrolled a lemonade stand.

Until then, I suppose "not evil" will have to do.

Old Wives vs. New Science

DON'T MAKE ME CHOOSE

I'M FED UP WITH scientists and their "indisputable findings" and their "absolute truths." It's all so vexingly inflexible.

Everywhere you turn there's another scientific study confirming that everything we know to be true — the conventional wisdom that society has for centuries held sacred — is, in fact, a load of bunk.

Just look at recent headlines. Cough medicine bad for kids. ... Multivitamins linked to cancer. ... Vitamin C no match for common cold.

Is nothing sacred to these hypothesis-happy lab dwellers?

I realize they're just doing their jobs, "saving lives," "making the world a better place," et cetera, et cetera. But must they keep undermining my confidence as a parent?

Here's the thing: We moms and dads are certain of so few things in life. Whether to let our kids express themselves or ask them to keep their voices down.

Whether to rescue them from a mean soccer coach or require them to honor their commitment to the team.

There are certain adages, though — not facts, mind you, but age-old aphorisms — that shore up our self-assurance in the kid-rearing arena. They prove that even if we're not, say, smarter than our kids, at least we've logged enough hours on this planet to have a non-slip grip on the vox populi: Bubble gum takes seven years to digest. Coffee stunts your growth. Pop Rocks and Coke make your stomach explode.

Reading in poor light will make you blind. Sitting too close to the TV will make you blind. Reading while sitting too close to the TV will just kill you outright.

But aside from a couple of key points that turn out, miraculously, to be true — basically, don't stare at the sun and keep the blow-dryer out of the bath water — most of our trusty rules of thumb are odiously bogus.

Get this: Hydrogen peroxide is actually not recommended for treating wounds, and the best way to take off a Band-Aid (come again?) is niiiice and sloooow.

Drinking milk does not increase mucus. Brushing hair is not good for it. Feed a cold, but never starve a fever. And go ahead, take a wild leap into the swimming pool right after you eat.

What is this? Bizarro parenting?

It's anarchy is what it is.

Clearly these mad scientists don't have children, or they'd know how crucial it is for parents to cultivate a voice of authority, even when we have no idea what we're talking about. If word gets out that our trusty truisms are nothing more than dusty old wives' tales, not even an apple a day will keep the backtalk away.

To be fair, though, science does occasionally work in our favor. For years, doctors have been poo-pooing the grandmotherly prediction that if you don't bundle up in brisk weather, you'll catch a cold. Two years ago, researchers in Wales finally proved it: Being cold and wet, they said, lowers our immunity, making us more susceptible to viruses.

This should be heartening news for those of us rendered parentally impotent by the distressing hydrogen peroxide smackdown. It means that even if we don't always know right from wrong, at least our grandmas did.

Remember, then, to stay toasty this winter. Chug coffee, if you like. Plop down with your nose to the TV screen. Swallow bubble gum instead of vitamins. Science condones it.

But if I were you, I'd avoid the Pop Rocks. Just in case.

Swearing Off New Year's Promises

IF YOU'VE EVER hauled your butt out of bed for a wailing infant, you know kids can be great motivators.

If you've relinquished a weekly manicure to save for their college, hand-scrubbed a kitchen floor just so they could crawl on it, or been unnaturally kind to a telemarketer because your progeny were standing there listening — then you've seen firsthand how effectively children can agitate for change.

I recently re-learned this concept. The hard way.

I was chauffeuring my 2-year-old home from day care when the driver of a slow and sloppy pick-up truck lurched his vehicle in front of mine and slammed on his brakes to turn into a driveway without using his signal. I cursed, as any safety-conscious mother might. And what I called the gentleman was not nice, I grant you that. But neither was the sound of my toddler's teeny-tiny voice echoing the four-letter sentiment from our back seat.

And with chilling gusto.

He repeated the phrase all the way home, as if it were the prettiest string of letters ever to alight on his eardrums. He shouted it. He whispered it. He sang it. And then he greeted his Daddy with it at the door.

Now I had made some ambitious resolutions for the coming year: I was going to get my infinite photos into albums, schedule a weekly date night with my husband and wake up an hour early every day to do a Pilates video. (Yes, I'm serious and I don't appreciate your snickering.)

But with my son's utterly age-inappropriate utterance, those plans flew out the #@¢%ing window. I had a new goal demanding my focus: I resolved to stop swearing in front of my children.

And I knew it wouldn't be easy.

Because even as our kids inspire us toward self-betterment — even as they challenge us to be cheerful, multi-tasking superhumans or else suffer the grueling guilt of failure — they also impede us from it, leaping into our paths like slow-moving, stubborn pick-up trucks. They're adorable little cogs in the works, sucking up money, time, and energy faster than they can drain a juice box at a post-game pizza party. Most moms will tell you they never had so many goals — and so little shot at actually accomplishing them — as they have since becoming parents.

And never is that paradox more pronounced than at New Year's. Resolutions promise a fresh start, a chance to finally fix the faults we've been unable to get our grocery-saddled and laundry-laden arms around so far.

And even if it's all a dirty little lie, we relish the fantasy of a life that's neater, happier, healthier. More guilt-free. A life that looks more like we pictured it would be, with everything in its proper place, ample time for spousal romance and abs that would never dream of flopping over our waistbands as we bend down — sigh — to kiss our perfectly behaved children goodnight.

There are certain annual rituals that moms cherish: Fourth of July fireworks, back-to-school shopping, pumpkin carving. But many of us feel about New Year's the way single folks feel about Valentine's Day: Why assign a special date just to make us feel bad about ourselves when we're capable of feeling that way all year long, and with little help?

So I propose we all go a little easier on ourselves this year. Sure, I'm still hoping to diffuse my internal F-bomb. But there's something more important I want to teach my kids in 2008: That despite what any dictionary tells them, "guilt" is a four-letter word.

Mothering the Mothers

AT THE SINKS, a trio of women recline side-by-side, eyes closed in seeming ecstasy as their locks are lovingly lathered. Two more ladies slump limply over massage chairs as therapists knead their necks and shoulders, tug gently on their arms, and roll rounded knuckles down their spines.

At the back of the salon, still more women sip mimosas and nibble lemon tarts as strangers caress their feet and drag brushes of "Zsa Zsa" polish across their newly buffed toenails.

This is living. This is the way to treat a lady. And yet ... you wouldn't want to trade places with a single one of them.

"All of these women have children with cancer," said Robyn Howard-Anderson, a pediatric social worker at Cottage Hospital. The pamper party is a gift from Walter Claudio Salon and the Teddy Bear Cancer Foundation, a nonprofit that gives financial and emotional support to the families of kids with cancer.

At the first of what may become an annual event, 50 mothers showed up to bask in a kindness that has become all but foreign to them as they trudge through the trials that cancer demands: the sucker-punch of diagnosis, the terrifying whirlwind of treatment, the guarded relief of remission, the deep fear of relapse, and, for some, the inconceivable devastation of loss.

Many of the mothers know each other. They hug and offer updates of their children's progress. Close-knit as they've become, though, theirs is a club formed by cruel, inscrutable circumstance. A club to which they — like all of you reading this — never imagined they'd belong to. A club with which some of them may never fully identify with.

"I still don't like to say the word cancer," said Santa Maria mom Debbie Goeres. After doctors found a malignant tumor on her 14-year-old daughter Kelsey's kidney, the family endured two years of stressful — but ultimately successful — treatment.

"You just could never, ever know what it's like to see a child suffer like that. Losing her hair and eyelashes, wondering if she was ever gonna eat again or look the same again," said Goeres, who lost 10 pounds herself in the first two weeks after Kelsey's diagnosis. "Stress can really do weird things to your body. Heart palpitations. High blood pressure. Insomnia. I had it all."

And while a facial and pedicure aren't exactly antidotes, they are very much welcome. "I do kind of feel like I deserve it," she said, smiling. "When you're going through something like that, you think it's never gonna end. And here we are."

But some aren't here for long. Despite her efforts to grin and be grateful, a woman whose 16-year-old son just relapsed with leukemia finds herself in tears and leaves the party. She can't do this today. For her, it's not time to relax. Not time for finger sandwiches and emery boards. It's time to be vigilant. To steel herself. To pray.

Oxnard resident Corrina Rubio has been there. The single mother of six lost her son Marcus last year just before his ninth birthday. He had a rare form of cancer that's seldom detected until it's too late to beat. Marcus underwent treatment for two years, including two stem cell transplants and countless trips to Los Angeles hospitals. "The disappointments, test after test," recalled his mother. "I'm thankful to have been there for my son every step of the way."

She's having her toenails painted pink today. She asked her teenage daughters to watch the younger kids, she tells me with a giggle. She told them she didn't know when she'd be home.

"This would be something I would never, ever do," she said. "You just don't think of treating yourself. It's really nice. But it's hard because you know why you're here. We're all going through the same thing, and we're trying to move forward."

Do You Have to Like Your Kids?

I WAS SWADDLED in nursing bras and burp cloths when a married-and-childless friend came to visit me and my 6-month-old. I needed the company. And she needed answers.

Emotionally, she felt the pull of parenting. But intellectually, she had doubts.

"What if you have kids," she asked, tentatively, "and you don't like them?"

She flinched when she said it, as though the words might puncture and deflate our friendship. She didn't know that a mere hour prior I had been explaining to my drooling neo-human that if he and I were going to get along, he would need to cease from spitting up in my hair.

"You really don't need to worry about that," I chuckled.

"Because when they're yours," she reasoned, "you can't help but like them … right?"

"No!" I said. "Because you most certainly will dislike them. Frequently. Intensely, even. And it won't matter much."

It was the first time I heard anyone give voice to that quiet little corner of the parenthood puzzle — the notion that a mother, the person we expect to love us unconditionally, might not like us unconditionally.

In fact, she might find us obnoxious.

It's a taboo topic, but any mom who has thought to herself, "I like them best when they're asleep," or has stared curiously while her 2-year-old stomped, shrieked and swatted his way through a grocery-store tantrum, has come to this inevitable conclusion: It's possible to live with someone — even to create someone — whose company you don't find especially charming.

"I do not always like my children," says a friend whose 10-year-old daughter recently told her she should wear more make-up.

"I don't like them when they stink," admitted another friend, a mother of boys. "I don't like them when they say, 'Why are you talking to dad like that?' And I sometimes like my book better than I like them."

"What I hate more than anything is when they are judgmental or intolerant," added a girlfriend with teenage daughters. "That sends me straight for the bottle of vodka."

These are three women whom — I promise — you would consider to be amazing mothers if you knew them. The truth is we have a kaleidoscope of feelings for our kids: Love. Hope. Pride. If "Constant Unbridled Delight" isn't in the spectrum, don't sweat it. We choose our friends and spouses expressly for their likability — funny? smart? kind? — but we don't get to custom-blend our kids' behavioral traits. And some of them, frankly, suck.

Take the Florida teen who was arrested for deliberately spiking her mother's dinner and sending the poor allergenic woman into anaphylactic shock. Mom's probably not brimming with affection today.

But how do we address our feelings of, well, unfondness?

"My mom would say, 'I love you but I really don't like you much right now,'" says a mom I know, who takes a similar tack with her own brood. "I've told them they were no fun to be around. Or that being in the same room with them just wasn't working for me."

I'm a proponent of natural consequences. So when my kids' behavior becomes so selfish, unreasonable or insulting that I can't stand to be around them, I tell them so as I'm walking away. But to be honest, it doesn't feel great.

Another friend of mine — one I apparently chose for her brutal honesty — insists that it doesn't matter what words we use to describe our displeasure.

"Your kids are too busy watching everything you do to listen to a word you say," she reminds me. "If you want to like them more, be more likeable. They will probably follow suit."

Needless to say — sometimes I don't like my friends either.

Party Favor

ENOUGH WITH THE EXTRAVAGANZAS

I'M DOING SOMETHING utterly outrageous for my son's third birthday party this month. I mean completely over the top. In fact, I'm pretty sure all the moms will be copying me next year.

Here's what I'm doing: Almost nothing.

I know. Crazy, right? Kids' birthday parties today tend to be more high-concept galas than low-key shindigs, replacing the once-popular cake-and-presents model with the full-blown dog-and-pony show. Sites like BirthdaysWithoutPressure.org have sprung up to protest the trend, arguing that elaborate invitations and themes, inflated guest lists, wedding-scale entertainment and extravagant party favors make for stressed parents and spoiled kids.

"I'm tired of being exhausted and tense on my kid's birthday," admits a friend of mine. "Especially if it is pointless — which it is."

The woman spent six years trucking in horses and

hiring musicians for her daughter's parties only to discover afterwards that her kid "does not in fact remember the band or the pony or the fairytale castle or the pumpkin-patch trip. None of it." They can't even jar her memory with photos of the events, because they didn't shoot any. "We were too busy running around conducting games or passing out prizes."

My boys and I weren't invited to Suri Cruise's second birthday bash, which reportedly cost $100,000. But we've attended parties where the "favor" (a portable art set with paints, pastels, and brushes) was nicer than the gift we brought (a favorite paperback book).

And we went to a casual backyard party where guests could hug a screeching orangutan and ride an African bull elephant. The 5-year-olds weren't interested in the beasts; there was a far more enchanting bouncy house in the side yard.

Why do we go wild over kiddie birthday parties?

"When little Hannah has a princess bouncer and frost-your-own cupcakes at her party, and lucky Liam takes the whole class for a ride on a real fire engine, you sort of feel like you might need to step it up a little," says another mom I know, whose pet peeve is the guest goody bags that are *de rigueur* at modern kiddie fetes. "When we were kids — and yes, I realize I sound ancient — you were happy to get a homemade cupcake. Now you have to give kids a present for coming to your kid's party? What IS that?"

It's nonsense, that's what. And I'm over it. Sure, in the past, I've hand-delivered message-in-a-bottle invitations all over town for a pirate birthday, and manned game stations across the yard for a carnival party. But this year, I'm not playing the one-up-manship game with my fellow party-planning parents. I'm setting the bar back at the bottom — down where my pre-schooler can actually reach it — with a simple backyard scamper fest. No inflatable jumpers. No themed tablecloth or dazzling Disney centerpiece. No piñata, magician or face-painter. The only entertainment I'm hiring is Duncan Hines to work his Supermoist magic on my son's fuss-free single-layer cake.

Even my gal pals who typically throw Birthday Extravaganzas have lauded my newfound laziness.

"I know my kids feel very special to receive the royal treatment," says a friend who once threw a Harry Potter party with a sorting hat, potion station, life-size chess board, wand-making table, sorcerer's stone hunt and backyard Quidditch match. "The problem is that each year we feel the need to either top the previous year or declare a 'pass,' as if the birthday isn't as important this year. I find myself praying I don't have to host a Star Wars Bar Mitzvah complete with R2D2 serving the food!"

Feelings of maternal inadequacy have no place in party planning. They're uninvited guests and should be blown out like birthday candles or popped like balloons.

If you thrive on throwing birthday banquets, knock yourself out. But those of us who have to answer to our envious invitees would ask that you toss a little restraint into your goody bags from time to time.

At least that's a favor we can all enjoy.

Growing by Bleeps and Bounds

MY FOUL-MOUTHED TODDLER

IT'S AN INCONGRUOUS sound. Like a parrot's squawk coming out of a puppy's mouth. Or a teddy bear that mutters "Life is pain" when you press its tummy. But there it is: My 2-year-old's face — eyes the size and shape of quarters, lips like red licorice — cussing like a trucker.

Through some terrible mutation of natural law, a four-letter word has become my young son's all-time favorite utterance. And not just a four-letter word. *The* four-letter word. The one usually reserved for sailors, inmates, and the occasional Vice President.

He used it at the park while, um, asking another child to kindly vacate his fort. He used it at home to inform some guests — with dramatic emphasis — that his favorite color is blue. And then, dear god, he used it at preschool.

He was sitting at the lunch table with friends when he let it rip. Finding the sound delightful, his buddies started shouting it, too. Their teacher explained that it was unacceptable language, and then called their parents to alert them to the special new phrase that — thanks to my just-out-of-diapers hooligan — might find its way to their otherwise G-rated dinner table that night.

Please, I asked the teacher, my cheeks hot with shame. Please tell me this wasn't the first time you've heard a child say this in your 8,000 years of teaching. Alas, she had only heard it once before. And it was from an older child. And it was in the 1970s "when," she explained, "everyone was using that word."

How was this possible? How could my offspring, so new to the world and yet so often lauded for his eloquent vocabulary, have turned into Andrew Dice Clay before he has even mastered the spoon?

Since I don't know where else the child could have picked up such an ugly habit, I'm blaming his preschool teacher, the most nurturing, kind-hearted and apparently foul-mouthed woman in the world. I picture her leading the class in "The Wheels on the Bleeping Bus" — not because she'd ever do it but because it makes me feel less culpable in my son's embarrassing outburst.

Short of soap in the mouth (because, frankly, it didn't work when my mom did it to me), we've tried everything to delete the word from his lingo. We gave him a substitute "naughty word" — "flush monkey" — but he isn't buying it. No one ever screams "flush monkey" when they get cut off in traffic.

One night, I encouraged him to say the expletive over and over again, hoping it would eventually lose its impact and we could move on with our generally unvulgar lives. Funny thing about that word, though; it just keeps getting better the more you say it.

Imagine, if you were just beginning to wade into the English lexicon, how exciting it would be to stumble upon a string of letters with such power. A word that makes people gasp, and giggle. A word that means so many things, and nothing at all.

"A little boy probably enjoys throwing around the word for the same reason he likes to shoot a cap gun," said my friend Mott, who's rather fond of the word himself. "He gets to wield a tiny bit of intensity in a mostly harmless way." A linguistics major, Mott also explained to me how the word's fricative beginning and commanding velar stop make it irresistibly fun to say.

As a writer, with an affinity for the subtle nuances of language, I'm loathe to decry certain words as "bad" and others … wait a minute. Did my friend just say "fricative"? Right here in my column? What does he think this is, the '70s?

The Third-Grader's Guide to Girls

THINGS WERE SO MUCH simpler when girls had cooties. Back then, my son's only interest in Valentine's Day was the promise of foil-wrapped chocolates and the pride of committing his herky-jerky signature to the race car-shaped Valentine cards he would hand out in class. But this year, something is different. The skirt-wearing, hair-twirling half of his class — the half once shunned at all the best birthday parties — is suddenly my son's favorite topic of conversation.

He doesn't especially want to talk about girls; he wants me to explain them to him. The way he and his 9-year-old buddies see it, the freckled coquettes who sashay around the schoolyard are dazzling but exasperating enigmas. They talk too much and never say anything that makes sense. They're pushy. They're pretty. They're pint-sized, pony-tailed puzzles with flavored ChapStick and Hello Kitty pencil cases.

All of which is how — when I would have preferred to

be doing something wholesome and escapist like helping him lick Valentine envelopes or scarf chocolates — I came to spend the week answering for my gender. My ruthless, diabolical gender.

Mom, why do girls act so cool? It's like they think girls rule or something. Okay, you didn't hear this from me, but girls do rule. We just do it in a sneaky way that makes boys think they're actually in charge.

How come girls are nice to me one day, then kick me in the shins the next? Sweetheart, girls are — hmmm, how to put this — lunatics. The Dr.-Jovial-and-Ms.-Snide act is a test we issue to see how much abuse you'll put up with before throwing up your hands and deciding to eat lunch with some other playground floozy. If you tattle on us, shove us or call us annoying, we know you're not really committed to the friendship. If, however, you stick it out and let us empty the contents of our naturally occurring schizophrenia onto your poor shins, you've won our loyalty forever. What we fail to tell you, though, is that the prize is actually … more shin-kicking.

Is one of girls' main goals to look pretty? Oh, heavens, no. The main goal is to get your attention and to keep you fixated on us, google-eyed, until your retinas burn from lack of blinking. Looking pretty is simply the easiest way we've found to do that.

Why do they like to style their hair so crazy, putting chopsticks through it, making pony tails all over their heads? Like boys, girls worry about how we will be perceived by the world. Will we seem smart? Fun? Creative? Strong? Unlike boys, we are under the impression that we can overhaul our image simply by altering our hair. We believe we can be tough-as-nails tomboys one day and four-foot femme fatales the next, merely by moving our part from left to right. This is a powerful conviction that must never, ever be challenged out loud. If a girl comes to school with string cheese braided into her mane, the proper response is, "Your hair looks nice that way."

Why do boys always seem to be the chasers, and girls the ones being chased? Because girls are better at disguising their boy-chasing (see shin-kicking, above).

Why do girls always start blabbering off? Any time of day, their brains are coming up with something for their mouths to say. Like the Sirens in Greek mythology, whose enchanting song caused distracted sailors to crash their ships into the rocks, girls hope to mesmerize you with our lilting, looping chatter. If you listen closely, you can learn what we care about, what scares us, what qualities we like most in a friend. Sometimes, though, you simply can't afford the distraction. Odysseus and his shipmates used earplugs to block the Sirens' call. And hey, if it worked for them …

Spring Cleaning

AND OTHER LIES
MEANT TO TORTURE US

"MOM, CAN I DRAW on my neck?"

It was spring and I was cleaning the kitchen — trying in vain to scrape the perpetual gick from the bottom of my toaster and scrub the perennial gunk from the base of the faucet — when I heard those words and glanced up, sponge in hand.

Indeed, my toddler's palms, forearms, elbows, T-shirt and the tablecloth surrounding his untouched coloring book were lavishly scrawled with shamrock-green marker.

"And," he was good enough to ask, "my hair, too?"

With that guileless question, a realization hit me bluntly, the way an upended dish of ice cream or an overturned bowl of oatmeal hits the floor (which it does frequently in our house): As long as there are children living here — and let's just say it, boy children to boot — my home will never ever be clean. Not for one hour. Not for one minute. Not for the split second it takes a 2-year-old to uncap a fat green marker.

While I lean less toward the white-glove school of housekeeping and more toward the sweep-it-under-the-rug approach, my predicament is universal. Households with kids just don't stay spit-polished the way adult dwellings do. It's simple math. Playground sand + Lego obsession + inability to master a fork = insurmountable sty.

Why, then, are we breeders burdened with the delusion of spring cleaning?

Why do parents' magazines and Target circulars and the commercials during *Desperate Housewives* keep insisting it's time to stock up on fresh-smelling cleansers and under-bed boxes and all-purpose microfiber cloths?

What, pray tell, would be the point?

If I followed my kids around all day with a spray bottle and a roll of paper towels, obliterating a syrupy handprint here and a muddy footprint there, I would only have to do it all again tomorrow. Aside from preparing lunch, any job that must be repeated daily is a form of torture — like Sisyphus forced to push his onerous, downward-tending boulder up the mountain.

Are the gods angry at us parents? Are we being punished with this yearly nudge toward neatness? Or is "spring cleaning" just a cruel marketing ploy by the same sadists who brought us New Year's resolutions, Valentine's Day and Lent (OK, that one's been around a while) — annual rituals designed to make us feel feckless and feeble-willed?

Show me the genius who coined the phrase "spring cleaning" and I'll show you a childless ad exec with a live-in maid.

Forgive me if I sound angry. I'd brandish a little more tact and diplomacy if only I could find them. But they're buried beneath piles of ketchup-stained laundry. Or they may be jammed at the back of the fridge behind that sticky bottle of Magic Shell from the great sundae party of 2003. I really can't remember the last time I saw them.

I adore the *idea* of spring cleaning, the promise, however cruel and deluding, that it's possible to clear out all the cobwebs and, um, dog hair, that collects in the corners of our lives. And I am envious — as green, in fact, as my son's graffiti'd arms — when I see other people's gleaming baseboards, steam-cleaned carpets and organized Tupperware drawers. I'm only human.

But those things are not attainable in my house. Not in this decade. Not while there are necks to be scribbled on. They're just a few of the many infeasible ideals of motherhood that collect, unnoticed, in the corners of my life.

If you come across one while attempting to tidy your roost this spring, I recommend you do what I do: Sweep it under the rug.

The Game of LIFE

FROM RAGS TO RICHES WITH A ROLL OF THE DICE

ONE MINUTE YOU'RE a Nobel Prize-winning doctor pulling in six figures. The next you're holed up in an aluminum-sided mobile home and your car's been stolen. LIFE is funny that way.

Not real life, so much. But we can all have a good chuckle when such twists of fate befall our limbless little game pieces in Milton Bradley's classic family board game, The Game of LIFE.

Now and again, my son and I take a spin around the old gameboard, taking equal glee in its little plastic churches and universities, its molded green mountains and the omnipotent spinner that (click! click! click!) launches players into outrageous fortune or calamitous destitution depending solely on the torque of one's thumb and forefinger.

Game nights let my kid and me bond over something besides *American Idol* ("Yes, his song choice was dope, son, but his performance was all a bit cabaret"). And they're educational, too. During a recent game, I learned that fantasy play is a pleasure one never really outgrows.

It's just that the fantasies change. And change dramatically.

Created in 1860 by Mr. Milton Bradley himself, the game was originally called The Checkered Game of Life. It promised players a "happy old age" if they made virtuous choices along the temptation-fraught path from infancy to infirmity.

Its modern incarnation, The Game of LIFE, was created in 1960 for the company's 100th anniversary. It has been updated a few times; today it rewards players for biking to work and helping the homeless, and docks their pay for having cosmetic surgery and buying high-def TVs.

But as time inches forward, like a game piece creeping across the board, social ideals aren't the only things about LIFE that change. I've noticed that as we players plod from childhood to adulthood, the game's entire appeal shifts.

For my fourth-grader, it's all about ownership: Holding, counting, and fanning out his rainbow of play money. Buying stocks and real estate, and fingering the deeds. In our latest game, he obsessively studied the fine print on his insurance policy and meticulously paid back his student loans when they came due. Along the path of LIFE, he collected all the symbols of adulthood he could wrap his 9-year-old fists around: a spouse, two kids, a boxy car. Basically, he had my life.

And I, quite deliberately, did not.

Because for me, the fantasy that LIFE affords is not in managing assets, changing careers, and hoping you can hold out till pay day. That's not entertainment; that's called "your thirties."

For me, the game's allure is freedom. The liberty to do it all over again — but less cautiously. To wit, I skipped college entirely and married a woman (less hair in the sink). A fateful spin of the wheel sent us skidding right past the treacherous "Baby boy!" and "Baby girl!" spaces on the board, protecting us from costly day care costs down the road. The wife and I shacked up in a modest log cabin without a shred of home insurance, or prudence, or even guilt. And we were deliriously happy, at least till that tornado hit.

All told, my delight in the game isn't so different from my son's. We both relish the chance to do things we can't do in real life, and to do them in a fail-safe environment.

Despite my lackadaisical approach to finances, I think I won that game. It's hard to know for sure because determining a victor is a complicated process requiring more math than anyone should have to do at 8:30 at night. If I have any criticism of this otherwise superbly escapist pastime, it's that after a long and colorful road full of unexpected twists and surprising developments, the end is an anti-climactic hassle.

But hey, isn't that LIFE?

Phantom Tiara Syndrome

THERE ARE THINGS I can't tell my family. Things they wouldn't understand. They don't know, for example, that elbow-length satin gloves make me warm and tingly inside. They've never noticed how my eyes go swirly-girly at the mention of glass slippers or fairy wings. They're entirely ignorant of my impeccable "Little Mermaid" impression — a spot-on vocal triumph charting every sigh, giggle, and vibrato of the brilliant girl-power ballad "Part of Your World."

You see, I'm the only female in my family of four. Where I grasp at magic wands, my husband and sons grab for laser guns. Where I dream of horse-drawn carriages, they drool over horse-powered muscle cars.

As I learned during a recent family excursion, nowhere is this disparity of passions more pronounced than at Disneyland.

A Southern California native, I spent an immoderate portion of my youth at the Happiest Place on Earth being merrily mesmerized by Disney's feminist-infuriating princess stories and blithely buying into the seductive sales arm of the operation: the Sparkly Princess Aesthetic.

To this day I can't park my car in the Pinocchio lot before my Pavlovian inner princess starts salivating: Tinker Bell tank tops? Hot pink tiaras? Dopey! Sneezy! Hold me back!

Like life, though, a trip to the Magic Kingdom is an entirely different tale when you're surrounded by boys. Sleeping Beauty's castle is merely that thing you have to tear through to get from the Astro Blasters, where you can shoot things, to the spinning teacups, where it's fun to make vomit jokes and watch Mom turn green.

We ride rocket ships. We buy swords. We watch an Indiana Jones look-alike beat the holy grail out of some swarthy, grunting bad guy.

And then I see it. Something new in the park: The Princess Fantasy Faire. We're marching off toward some unsparkly treehouse or another when I spot a shady enclave where little girls are decorating crowns, dancing with knights, and curtsying before tiny-waisted Cinderella and big-haired Belle.

"Oh, GOD," my husband announces. "Aren't you glad we don't have to wait in those lines?"

What I say is, "Phew. You're tellin' me."

What I'm thinking is, "Remember that hour we spent at the Jedi Training Academy? That's 60 minutes of my life I'll never get back."

What I'm singing in my head is, "What would I give if I could live out of these waters?... Wandering free, wish I could be part of that world."

To be fair, there are advantages to mothering boys. Though I've had to abandon pre-parenthood fantasies of delicate tea parties and shopping expeditions for sequined sandals (not for lack of trying but because my sons won't humor me), I maintain hope that some day my new-found ability to distinguish a backhoe from a front-end loader will prove wildly useful.

The best part of being the lone gal in a house full of guys is the sort of confused reverence with which you are viewed. As everything about me is different — my body, my talents, my passions — I'm seen as somewhat mysterious. Complicated. Special. Surrounded on three sides by "he"-hood, I get to be the lone shore of "she"-hood. The very model of femininity. The fairest, in effect, of them all.

At the end of our Disneyland day, I drag my 2-year-old to the princess-heavy Parade of Dreams, so I — rather, so he — can see doe-eyed damsels float by, waving their gloriously gloved fingers in that fluid, inhuman way.

He is bored and fidgety till his eyes lock onto Tinker Bell, flapping her fairy wings and flicking her pixie stick at the crowd. But the look on his face isn't enchantment — it's faint recognition.

He points at the life-size fairy and wrinkles his nose. "Is that Mommy?" he asks…

And we live happily ever after.

Who Wants to Be a Cotillionaire?

I WOULDN'T WANT you to think etiquette has no place in my home. We are not heathens.

When I belch triumphantly at the dinner table and blame it on my son, he always, always, says, "Excuse me."

Still, we are not the very paragons of poise. And thus I was thunderstruck last fall when my 8-year-old asked if he could join his school chums at cotillion.

I didn't know what cotillion was, and all efforts to find out only further befuddled me, defined as it is by inscrutable terms like "debutantes," "polite society," "social graces," and something called "niceties."

Turns out cotillion is an old-school manners camp that obliges children — who have only recently mastered the art of shoe-tying — to dress up like fusty little mortgage lenders and practice chivalry, obsolete dance steps, and the fine art of balancing a cookie, party napkin, and glass of punch on one's wiggly, wobbly lap.

None of which should be remotely appealing to a

third-grade boy. But my son wanted to wear a suit so he could look like James Bond. He was curious about how boys are expected to interact with girls once they're done shooting spitballs at them. And, ultimately, my crafty little hooligan convinced me to enroll him in the expensive, elitist, and antiquated class by appealing to my knee-jerk maternal fantasies.

"Mom, if I'm ever invited to the White House for dinner, I'll feel so uncomfortable," he pleaded, "unless I've been to cotillion."

So we shelled out for the obligatory traditional dark suit, thin-soled dark leather oxfords, and gentleman's standard tie. (The dress code asks even parents to sport "Country Club attire at minimum," typed just like that, with initial caps, as if country clubs were a geographical entity unto themselves.)

The grown-up hostesses wear Grace Kelly cocktail dresses with pearl chokers, their hair curled into ringlets. One is a former beauty queen. The hosts grin like Ken dolls and chuckle far more than is called for. In sing-songy, Stepfordy voices, they beseech their 8- to 11-year-old charges to line up, boy-girl-boy-girl, and do the cha-cha-chá.

"Hands out of your pockets, gentlemen!" they caution. "Make sure and smile, because even if you're nervous on the inside, no one else needs to know ..."

The boys learn to approach girls — dressed in "modest" frocks and short white gloves — and ask them to dance. They must learn their partners' full names, and introduce them to neighboring couples on the dance floor. They practice applauding and thanking their hosts for a lovely party. They learn to "cut in" on another couple's dance, to lead their partner to a metal folding chair, and to sit down on her left without ever — I kid you not — showing her their backside. (It's worth mentioning that the National League of Junior Cotillions lists Donald Rumsfeld among its Best Mannered People.)

Not surprisingly, my Bond wannabe doesn't love cotillion. One day, I watched him take his dance partner's empty cup and napkin to the trash and return to her side, clumsily retrieving her gloves from his suit pocket while she consulted with a nearby girlfriend as to whether she had chocolate on her face. He rolled his eyes. Afterward, he told me the experience had been off-puttingly "fancy prancy" and even, I'm sorry to say, "fruitsy-tootsy."

Which is fine with me, since I've never enjoyed nor trusted men whose MO is the same behavioral code their grandfathers used to get their grandmothers into the sack.

I give props to cotillion, though, for teaching my son — perhaps unintentionally — that there are people in life who will judge him solely on his manners.

Mostly I'm grateful that if he does wind up dining at the White House with a high-bred debutante, and feels the need to belch, he'll have the good sense to blame it on her.

Flights of Fancy

A LETTER TO FIRST-CLASS PASSENGERS

DEAR FRONT-OF-THE-PLANERS,
    Let us introduce ourselves. We are those less-fortunate passengers who shuffle humbly past you toward the back of the plane, trying not to bump your proud shoulders with our awkward-sized carry-ons. Ultimately, we have the same destinations as you: Des Moines. O'ahu. Düsseldorf. But for now, we're headed toward seats bolted so close together they might as well be spooning. Seats designed for people the size of Mary-Kate Olsen.

You go out of your way to avoid eye contact with us as we pass you, and we can't blame you, really. Having been invited to board early, you're deep, and I mean deep, into your SkyMall catalog and can't tear your eyes from that Solar-Powered Mole Repeller. Sure. We get it.

Just so you know, though, we are looking at you. Checking you out from your smug face down to your exorbitant leg room. And we have something to tell you.

Yes, ladies and gentlemen, the captain has just turned off the no-bitching light, so get your eminent damned ears in their full upright position. We want to explain why we coach castaways are bitter about this whole two-caste seating arrangement. We want you to know why our resentment is at an altitude of 10,000 feet — and climbing.

Summer is travel time for Americans of all class distinctions, from those who've saved all year for the privilege of staying in some thin-walled motel room near a brat-teeming theme park to those who'll be genuinely affronted when the bath towels in their Paris penthouse are faux Frette.

But airplanes don't allow all types of vacationers to mingle. We airfare-scroungers are sequestered from you by a symbolic mesh curtain the flight attendants fling open and closed with extraordinary dramatic flair.

What on earth is going on up there? Medical exams? Bikini waxes? Lap dances?

Financially, maybe even socially, our two "cabins" are worlds apart. But actually, we're sitting quite near you. We hear your real silverware clinking on your real china plates as we use our flaccid plastic knives to pry the Saran-wrapped dinner rolls out of our Snak Paks.

We hear the stewardess — the same woman who just rolled her eyes when we asked for extra peanuts — offer you a bread basket with your meal. We hear her offer you a pillow. And a refill of shiraz. Now it's coffee. Good god, does the woman ever shut up? We're glad she doesn't bug us all the time like that.

In truth, we know you're not any happier than we

are. Linen napkins and elbow room notwithstanding, time spent in first class is still wasted time. When we hit turbulence, is your ride less bumpy than ours? When we are late taking off, are you not late, too? When first-class toddlers kick the back of your seat, are you not just as inclined to send them outside to play?

And though our coach-class keisters are not allowed to touch your hoity-toity ... um ... toity, we know your lavatory is no less a poorly lit, germ-slick torture chamber than ours.

But it's attitudes, not amenities, that make commercial air travel tolerable. And while we can see how VIP treatment would make you feel better about being stuck in an aluminum tube, we should warn you that staring at your elitist curtain hour after hour makes us cramped commoners cranky.

And as you exit the plane — ahead of us, naturally — remember that we are right behind you. And we are now united in our hostility toward you. And there are far more of us.

In other words, watch your pampered posteriors as you exit the aircraft, folks, as the balance of power may have shifted during flight.

My First Fisticuffs

**THE GOOD, THE BAD
AND THE BLOODY**

THE FIRST THING I noticed was how quiet it was. The experience was more like visiting an operating room than attending a sporting event.

I'd never seen a boxing match before, figuring it was one of those things like Sammy Hagar, or Jack Daniels, the enjoyment of which is reliant on a scrotum, or an unhappy childhood.

But a friend invited me to the Chumash Casino to watch five boxing bouts — they laugh at you if you call them "games," and it's not a friendly laugh. Since I had never seen a man punch another man in the face — something everyone should really witness once — I accepted.

Approaching the arena, I steeled myself for the male-specific pandemonium I expected to find inside: hooting, chest-thumping, and the hurling of paper beer cups for no apparent reason. And let me say in all fairness that the image was not unarousing.

But neither was it accurate.

Inside, hundreds of people — including women, some of whom appeared to be there by choice — sat silently and politely, fixated on the ring. The only sound was the soft, but consistent, "poof" of a leather glove slapping a sweaty pec, or skidding across a glistening shoulder (again with the arousal).

In fact, you could say my expectations suffered a KO from the first round. Where I had imagined rage, there was control. Where I had envisioned savagery, there was courtesy. A mutual admiration between the opponents of this "noble art," this "sweet science," was evident in the way they hold each other up when they need a rest, and hoist each other up when they win. Given the task at hand, though, the respect is almost chilling — like a hunter with a deep reverence for his prey.

Thank goodness there were sparkly pants to distract us. I developed a fondness for the satiny bloomers, embroidered with charming nicknames like "El Perro." One welterweight had pearls and fringe hanging from his boots. Who knew pugilistic couture could be so sassy?

Or patriotically sexy? The Ring Babes — a stable of nubile young women clad only in star-spangled bikinis and heels — parade around the ring between rounds. Supposedly they hoist signs over their heads that say what round it is, but this is unconfirmed because no one has ever bothered to look above their heads.

Boxing, though, isn't all hard bodies and flashy costumes. It's actually quite jarring to watch; ugly, even.

Backlit by an assault of klieg lights and sweat, dislodged mouth guards fly through the air. Between rounds, woozy players apply ice packs to their bruised ears, spit into funnels, and may receive verbal abuse or a smack in the head from a nervous coach.

Plus, there's the blood. When a guy's split eyebrow bleeds down his face and smears across his opponent's white shorts, the injured boxer stops looking like a focused athlete and starts looking like a wounded human. An unfortunately employed man-child. A victim of society's barbaric lust for base entertainment.

No one seems to smile at a boxing match. No matter who's winning, there's empathy on the face of every spectator, male or female, young or old, coach or fan, judge or sportscaster.

And that's because boxing is personal. The sport isn't played over a vast field or wide diamond; it's negotiated within the bright, humid inches between two hopeful, diligent strangers. It's not happening to a ball; it's being waged on the flesh of two meticulously sculpted bodies.

Since that's the case, I'd personally rather watch the Ring Babes have it out — a nice catfight where Raw Passion yanks Respect by the hair.

Call me a featherweight, but I think intent-to-maim should be aggravated and instinctual, rather than premeditated and emotionless.

At least when a chick decks another chick, you know it was cathartic for someone.

Numb and Number

I'M NO STRANGER to sedation.

As a teen, whenever the storm of adolescence would shudder through my soul and come surging out of my face in the form of sobs and tears, my mother would offer me Valium. She tried to pass it off as aspirin, assuming I didn't recognize the big ol' V carved into each tiny, white anxiety-quasher. I usually declined to take them, arguing a $20 bill and a ride to the mall would better serve my particular brand of woe. But once in a while, like after a gnarly breakup with a dreamy boyfriend, I'd gulp down my mother's little helpers and wait for the utterly undue, blessedly baseless calm it promised.

As a mother myself now, I don't use prescription downers — which may well be because I don't yet have teenagers. But I don't begrudge anyone whose life-coping strategy falls short of focused yogic practice and transcendental meditation. How could I, when my own stress elixir is a big spoon, a can of chocolate frosting, and a brain-deadening string of TiVo'd *Desperate Housewives* episodes?

I heard an ad on the radio yesterday, though, that surprised me (and in our increasingly tranquilized society, surprises are becoming rarer and rarer). It was a local dentist whose primary appeal to customers was that — whether they're getting a filling or a root canal — he will make sure they're good and sedated. "Imagine sleeping soundly through your entire dental procedure and waking up refreshed, with little or no memory of the visit," read the Web site, when I investigated further. "Most patients report having little or no memory of the experience, including sounds or smells!"

Optimal candidates, it reads, are people who have busy schedules, can't stand needles, and "hate the noises, smells, and tastes associated with dental care."

So that's pretty much everyone, right?

Don't get me wrong — I'm no freedom fighter in the war against drugs. Who doesn't crave a little mind-whacking chemical intervention when the day goes dreadfully wrong? When you're trying to finish a column, say, and your toddler is wailing about his menacing molars and your dog is trying to attack the poor FedEx guy and that freaking parking ticket is still laying on the kitchen counter unpaid and there's a war in Iraq that you really should be out somewhere protesting? If I had a bottle of Xanax in front of me right now, I might very well deplete it. Because even a privileged life can be nerve-jangling.

However — and not to be a Tom Cruise here because I honestly think the guy could use some sedatives — what's the cost of paving over all our bad feelings? How long before we, as a culture, can tamp down every anxiety we can name, from embarrassment to social nerves to those oh-so-unpleasant survival jitters that perk up when we're stuck in an elevator with a creepy weirdo?

Certainly prescription mood enhancers are a blessing for folks grappling with devastating life events, or the kind of psychological demons that stonewall one's ability to get through the day. But like any great drug, sedatives are becoming a health problem. Recent news stories report kids in Houston, Brooklyn, and Philadelphia have been hospitalized for addiction and overdose on downers like Xanax.

Then there's the more philosophical pickle: Isn't a little anxiety good for us? Doesn't it help us regulate our behavior in ways that keep us safe, healthy, and hassle-free? If the prospect of having our teeth worked on causes our ribcages to constrict around our lungs and racing hearts, we could seek out a Halcion-hyping hygienist. Or, we could resolve (ahem) to start flossing more. When the chaos of our lives bubbles to boiling and threatens to burst out through our throbbing temples, we could pop an Ativan. Or, we could see it as a sign we need to reprioritize.

I feel that sometimes strong emotions should be fully experienced, rather than numbed. I feel there's value in stress and lessons in fear. I feel the promise of pharmaceutical peace is as dangerous as it is appealing. Mostly, though, I'm just glad I can still feel at all.

Cyber Sleuthing

HE WAS THE BIGGEST EGOMANIAC I ever fell in love with. A stunning singer/songwriter in his sexual prime, Dave made fun of fat girls, carried a baseball bat in his car in case of trouble, and called my dear grandfather "Gramps" the first time he met him. He wore skirts in public just for the attention, and had me write his college entrance essay because hallucinogens had stymied his powers of concentration.

The last words he said to me were, "What, do you want me to treat you like a princess?" I figured anyone who couldn't puzzle that out was destined for failure in life.

But an ill-advised Internet search last month revealed that Narcissistic Acid-Head Dave is now ... um ... Dr. Dave, a heroic veterinarian who brings beasties back from the brink of death. An online newsletter lauds my ex-beau for saving Dewey, a Chihuahua foster puppy, by securing "little bone screws" on the mutt's "tiny leg." Further research revealed Dave lives with 18 pets and an astonishingly beautiful wife who clearly has no princess complex but (thank you, Google) does have a warrant out for her arrest.

All this cyber sleuthing was inspired by *Five Men Who Broke My Heart,* Susan Shapiro's nonfiction account of tracking down her greatest loves. My book club agreed to read the tell-all, then dig up dirt on our own former flames. I found the exercise addictive, dredging up ex-lovers' marriage licenses and wedding photos, charting their careers and offspring, spotting lies on their résumés and misspellings on their Web sites.

Thanks to Google, Classmates, Facebook, MySpace, and LinkedIn, you can now find almost anyone online — instantaneously and anonymously. But what you find is sometimes shocking.

A fellow book club member hunted down the nicest boy she ever dated, a Cornell architecture student. "I can't tell you how white-bread sweet he was," she said. These days, he's a dreadlocked, highly pierced tattoo artist who won TLC's *Tattoo Wars.* Another found that her "low-life" boyfriend, who worked at the I.V. co-op, is now a successful patent attorney.

"The guy I lusted after in high school?" said another friend. "Fat and bald."

The revelations aren't just fun — they're emotionally stirring.

"It makes you think about what your life would have been like if you stayed with that person," explained another friend of mine.

You may find yourself searching for clues in his life

that he never really got over you: Did he marry someone who looks like you, or name his kids what you always said you'd name them? And you can't help wondering — just for that one ugly moment — how he managed to accomplish any of this without you.

But why should we care what these also-rans are up to?

"Revenge? Comparison?" offers a friend. "I mean, I'm glad I'm not with him, but I'm even gladder if he doesn't own half of New York City or have pictures of him on his 200-foot yacht on his MySpace page. You know what I mean?"

Another gal said she finds comfort in seeing evidence of life-after-breakup. "It's a way to revise history," she said, "to prove it wasn't that bad after all. See? Everyone recovered."

If you decide to cyber snoop on a paramour, be prepared: A surprising number of them turn out to be gay. I can't explain this. It's just a thing.

And keep your peeping in the digital arena. "There's no harm in looking online," said a friend, "but if it goes beyond virtual and into actual reality, you've crossed over into bunny-boiling territory."

But that's nothing Dr. Dave couldn't handle.

Smellywood's Puttin' on the Spritz

I T'S BAD ENOUGH I have to read about Britney Spears's parenting failures in my entertainment magazines. I can't get through an issue anymore without facing a photo of the former teen queen's by-now-all-too-familiar upper thighs. Now — thanks very much — I have to smell her, too.

An acrid aroma emanated from the pages of my favorite mindless reading material recently, and I was as bewildered as repulsed by the sensation: something sinisterly sweet and nauseating, like a syrupy pink cocktail, that storms your sinuses and then jabs at the gag button at the back of your throat.

I know Britney's had a hard go lately, but I'm sorry: Is this what the girl smells like?

The potion is called *Believe*, and it comes in both a traditional spray and, um, "body soufflé." It's being hawked with an image of Britney's head on someone's much thinner body, and this motto: "I believe every woman needs a secret."

You know what I believe? I believe that's a funny mantra for a woman whose coochie is all over the Internet.

Celebrity perfumes are a billion-dollar industry. Sales of the top seven alone — led, inscrutably, by the former P. Diddy's *Unforgivable* — topped $350 million last year, according to market researchers. They may not be great scents, but business-wise, VIP vapors make great sense. It's hard for fragrance companies to convince consumers to sample — much less fall in love with, purchase, and commit the rest of their lives to wearing — some out-of-the-blue perfume, no matter how brilliantly its "top note" segues to its "dry down."

Eau de Superstar has built-in appeal, making star-watching saps feel like they're enveloped in their idols' auras. The logic: If we can't look like them, sing like them, dress like them, or — in the case of David Beckham's *Instinct* cologne — play midfielder like them, then at least we can offend people's olfactory glands like them.

But from a consumer standpoint, the notion stinks of stupidity. Consider that perfumes bear the names of Michael Jordan, a man famous for the various ways in which he generates sweat, and Kate Moss, a woman whose nasal passages have proven to be less than discerning.

I wonder why we've not seen a Keith Richards fragrance called *Undead*, with hints of embalming fluid and a soft whisper of old cigarettes. How soon before we can douse ourselves in Lindsay Lohan's *Rehab*, with the earthy essence of black coffee and Altoids?

Anyone who believes these stars actually wear their

namesake tinctures has been sniffing too much of Paris Hilton's *Heiress*. Mariah Carey recently confessed that she never even liked perfume until Elizabeth Arden slapped her name on a product called *M*, not to be confused with Gwen Stefani's *L*. (Tell me you wouldn't love to see Paris come out with an amber-colored eau de toilette called *P*.)

It's not personalities, or even lifestyles, that inspire these essences — it's cold, unscented cash. Celebs get 5 to 10 percent of the sales of each bottle that bears their name. J.Lo's perfume line (*Glow* reportedly smells like soap because she was fresh out of the shower during her first consultation with Coty) sold $77 million last year, netting her at least $4 million — nothing to sniff at.

Unlike the odor of Britney's *Believe*, though, the phenomenon shows signs of dissipating. Sales are expected to drop by 25 percent over the next three years as buyers, not all that smart to begin with, become confused by the overwhelming number of choices.

It's a good thing that oddball British actor Alan Cumming launched his signature scent when he did. Unlikely to be seen in magazine ads, his steady-selling elixir is a wink at the fact that sex, and celebrities, can sell anything. Its name: *Cumming*.

Down With Uptalk

I OWE YOU ALL a big apology.

Because when I was a kid? Growing up in the San Fernando Valley? We talked in this totally weird way and all? And, like, it spread.

More egregious than our senseless devotion to Vans slip-ons, more deplorable than our establishment of the Church of Mall, more reprehensible than our role in launching Moon Unit Zappa's "musical" career — we Valley Girls of the 1980s injected a hideous habit into the nation's lexicon.

It's the tendency to make every declarative sentence, every piddling phrase, sound like a question.

And it's only now that our kids are doing it that we can fully appreciate how utterly, vexingly brain-piercing it is.

So, like, someone's talking to you? And it's not like they're trying to sound moronic? But they can't really help it because they're caught in a sing-songy loop? From which escape ... is, like ... not likely?

Linguistic experts call these quips "high-rise terminals" for their upward intonation. But James Gorman, a journalism teacher at NYU, coined the term "uptalk" in 1993 after noticing his students doing it.

The verbal tic is associated with youth, but has been documented in high-profile adults from NPR's Terri Gross to President George Bush. And though its origin has been traced to Southern California, it's now common on the East Coast, and in Canada and Australia.

England, needless to say, is terrified.

While I confess to being more from the "yucky, make it stop" school of linguistic analysis, there are folks who actually try to figure out why such trends take hold. Some say kids haven't yet mastered the art of conversation and feel the need to check in with their audience at the end of each sentence; it's like saying, "Are you still listening?"

A fifth-grade teacher I know believes her students do it to buy time, to pause and collect their thoughts before proceeding with their story. But in a world where confidence is revered, uptalk can reflect negatively on a speaker's character.

"It says they're unable to take a stand, to make a definitive statement," says a friend of mine, whose brother-in-law is prone to it. It's also a passive-aggressive way of skirting censure, she says, as in, "We can't make it over to see you because we have this fancy party to go to?"

"You can't argue with a question," she points out ... "even if it isn't really a question."

A buddy of mine, a self-described linguistics geek, says the phenomenon's both natural and harmless. People use uptalk simply to identify with a cultural group: the cool kids at school, the surfer crowd in their community, the young folks in the office, etc.

We pass through different culture groups as we age, he says, and most people are able to "shift conversational registers" according to whom they are addressing. So your kids are no more likely to carry uptalk with them into the job market than they are to drag their favorite childhood blankie along.

Just to be safe, though, I recommend spending this summer breaking your kids of the habit. I know a second-grade teacher who reads to her students using uptalk so they can hear how absurd it sounds. My cousin simply asks her thoroughly exasperated daughter, "Was that a question? And if so, how do you expect me to answer it?"

My own parents — in an effort to ensure that when they took the girl out of the Valley, they could also shake the Valley out of the girl — simply mocked me by saying, "Uh-huhhhhh?" every time I paused to take a breath.

It may have been harsh, but I'm here to tell you it works. There's no question in my mind.

Email Embarrassment

GRAY SKIES. Sinus headache. Fresh out of coffee filters. It's a crappy morning.

Which is why, when you check your email and find an overly chipper note from an overly perky acquaintance, you are inspired to rant like Dr. Laura during a hot flash.

Your vitriol is not aimed directly at the emailer, of course. Technically, the buoyant broad has done nothing wrong. Technically, you can't fault her for sending that reminder about the school fundraiser, even if it does contain far too many exclamation points and all-capped words and phrases like "SUPER-FUN way to support our OUTSTANDING extra-curricular programs, and get a holly jolly jump on your holiday shopping, too!!!"

Technically — officially — you must respond with a note that matches her disturbing effervescence note for note. And you will. Right after you type a blistering tirade about this woman's acute and unnerving glut of glee (I think "Anyone who can get this excited about gift wrap needs her meds adjusted" are your exact words) and send it to your blessedly bitchy best friend.

At least, that's where you thought you sent it. But no sooner has the thing left your outbox than it strikes you: You don't recall hitting the "forward" button.

Oh, no no no no no. Sweet Jesus. You hit "reply."

And though that miniscule error took less than a second to make, the fallout is tremendous. Stomachs clench. Arm hair stands on end. And much audible gasping ensues, both on your side of the screen ... and on hers.

Never was the word "oops" more inadequate.

Because it's one thing to think like a shrew, and it's another thing entirely to type like one. Now you have exposed yourself as someone who is not only unsupportive of SUPER-FUN programs and recklessly indifferent to the holiday shopping rush, but duplicitous, too. And mean. And perhaps worst: technologically retarded.

Would that the world were more idiot-proof. If only email had an "un-send" option or a pop-up window that could safeguard us from our own stupidity by asking, "Are you sure you want to tear this person a new one?" before it would allow you to send.

Short of that, here are a few ways to recover when you inadvertently bitch slap someone via email.

1) Blame it on your children. How many times have we let ourselves get into trouble because we didn't take this easy, and relatively harmless, way out? People are amazingly forgiving of children, and let's face it, your kids probably did something bad at some point that they weren't blamed for, so it all works out karmically. Try this: "I'm so sorry. The 2-year-old was messing with my computer again and thought it would be funny to call you 'a self-involved strumpet who has yet to master the possessive apostrophe.' Personally, I didn't find it funny, and I told him as much."

2) Chalk it up to a virus. Not yours, but your computer's. (Although, if you can convince someone that bronchitis made you do it, I say go with that.) "Haven't you heard of the Insult virus?" you ask, with appropriate horror. "It infects your email and sends nasty messages to everyone in your address book. They seem so real, too. It called my boss a slave-driving weenie, but I guess if he can laugh it off, you can, too!"

3) Claim you're bipolar, and work the sympathy angle. "Ugh, I have to apologize. You caught me in my manic phase: impulsive, aggressive, quick to anger. But I want you to know I've purchased plenty of gift wrap to keep on hand for my next depressive state. If it can do for me what it did for you that would be REALLY SUPER!!!"

My New Stud

I T'S RARE THAT I wake up and decide that I should have a hole in my face where no hole should technically be. But last month, I arose to a profound and irrepressible urge to pierce my right nostril.

"Why would you do that?" my mother said frankly.

"You mean, like, permanently?" my husband asked cautiously.

"What about boogers?" my friends cautioned, understandably.

I couldn't explain it except to say that while most other piercings give me the big-time heebies, I've always thought a tiny diamond stud in the beak looks kind of exotic and pretty. Like an Indian princess. Or, well, Lenny Kravitz. A little razzle-dazzle with a fringe-culture flair. (And come on, how often does a girl get to be both sparkly and edgy at the same time?)

I teach on a college campus where students have more facial jewelry than freckles: lips, eyebrows, ear cartilage, the bridge of the nose, and now a freaky little stud called a "Monroe" or "Madonna" that mimics the cheeky beauty mark of its namesake style icons. On campus, one is made to feel unwhole for being unholey.

Surely my age factored into the decision. Call it a pathetic attempt to chase "hip," to cling to my youth. Call it a mid-face crisis, if you must. But grant me this: If I can no longer stave off fine lines and dark circles, can't I at least use bright, shiny objects to distract from them?

Because I dislike surprises, particularly when they manifest in the form of staph infections, I researched the hell out of nose piercing before I shuffled, alone and wobbly legged, into the tattoo and piercing parlor.

I learned, for example, that noses aren't pierced with a quick earring-style gun but with a more hygienic and terrifyingly long needle. The piercer sticks something corkish up your nostril for the needle to poke into. It's a truly unattractive process. (And, for the record, I recommend you do not watch piercing videos on YouTube as it will only cause your sphincter to contract.)

I surprised the piercer by choosing a gem twice the size of the recommended starter stud. Her argument was that it's best to start small, so you can get used to the look of it. My argument was that if I'm going to let a stranger slide a needle through my face — and pay her to do it, no less — I'd better have something significant to show for it.

It was painful, I won't lie. It hurt less than a tetanus shot (because it was faster) but more than having blood drawn (because it was rougher).

Other odd facts I discovered: Your eyes tear up

involuntarily when the needle goes through. It can take as many as six flipping months to heal. And rather than have backings like earrings, most studs simply have L-shaped posts that flop around awkwardly in your nose, occasionally poking down out of your nostril for all the world to stare at curiously before gasping and looking away in distaste.

The gem catches on things. Lots of things. Washcloths. The price tags on new sunglasses. Even, er, the nose of one's partner during passionate lip-locking sessions. Once, my 2-year-old announced, "No sparkly," and yanked it right out. Which felt exactly like you'd think it would.

But despite the hassle and hurt, I love this glinting new thing on my face. My once-wary mom even likes it. My husband thinks it's sexy in an Indian-princess-meets-Christina-Aguilera way. And I've been able to assure my more indelicate friends — without going into great detail — that boogers actually are not an issue. Really! It's the truth.

The hole truth.

I'm Virtually Popular!

MY COWORKERS MUST really love me. They share every detail of their lives with me — every snagged stocking and lost set of keys, every extended vacation and fundraising endeavor. They remind me when it's time to order business cards, invite me to join the basketball pool, and ask me if I saw the scamp who stole the stapler right off their desk.

Of course, most of them have no idea who I am. They wouldn't, in fact, recognize me if I were crouched naked on their desks humming the theme from *The Office*. Because while I'm employed by several companies, I don't occupy a cubicle at any one of them. I work at home, a freelance serf toiling solitarily at a cheap-ass desk in a drafty corner of my dining room.

But I'm connected to the staffs of various offices via group email announcements. So while I can't gather 'round the water cooler to discuss politics and gossip about office romances, I get to "hear" whenever a fellow employee is, say, looking for duct tape to fix his shoe. Which is weird. But it's not uncommon. Statistics show 45 million Americans worked at home in 2006, and the number's expected to top 100 million by 2010.

I used to work in an office: Ergonomic chair. Spontaneous donut days. All the Wite-Out I could burn through. A computer guy who brought me a new keyboard every time mine jammed up mysteriously (with donut crumbs). You could say I had the whole corporate caboodle. And I don't miss it.

I don't miss the traffic, the clock-watching managers, the "appropriate" attire, or the fancy phone system with its diabolical transfer button. But … it does get lonely working by myself. And it's a new kind of loneliness. An odd kind. Because thanks to the cyber miracle of the "send all" button, I'm still very much in the loop. Only it's not a person-to-person, I-really-value-your-input loop. It's a loop of endless, distant digi-chatter that makes me feel tragically isolated from colleagues even as I wish they'd shut up for 10 minutes and let me work.

To be fair, I sometimes welcome the distraction. And the chuckle. Like when a broken water main leaves the Santa Barbara City College restrooms "out of use." The faculty was recently notified, in all seriousness, that the Hula Hoop Club needed an adviser, and polled to see if anyone could shelter some French exchange students who needed little more than a bed each night and a croissant each morning.

Other times, office emails make me glad I don't spend my day functioning among other humans — snipey and apparently quite slovenly humans.

"When you (whoever you are) make coffee, please make sure it does not leak all over the counter — like it just did," read one recent email. Or: "The refrigerator is growing things. Oh, the smell! Please mark your food clearly if you don't want it thrown out. There will be no more reminders." And also: "Whoever owns the grey Prius, you'll need to move your car by the time I get back in an hour. You're in my spot."

Laboring solo while being privy to office action is like watching the world from behind a sound-proof, two-way mirror, like Jimmy Stewart in *It's a Wonderful Life*. The false connection is most disappointing when it offers up something cool ("Free Lakers tickets in my office. First one here gets 'em.") that offsite grunts like me can't have.

It's like chomping on a virtual donut — or bagel.

"Fresh apple butter in the kitchen for your bagels," taunted the cruelest, and most memorable, email. "Made by my mama in Michigan. Help yourself."

Would that I could, stranger. Would that I could.

A Croc of Shoe

WOULD YOU BUY a car called the Volkswagon Hoax? Would you dine at a bistro called Bilk? Or get your hair done at the Dupe Salon? Few would. And yet millions of people pay $30 a pair for the ugliest footwear ever to cradle a human heel — shoes whose very name is synonymous with "nonsense."

Crocs. They're a sham at the end of your shin. A prank below your ankles. A fraud perpetrated on the feet of fools.

There are few of us left on the planet who don't own a pair of the holey, rubbery, sea slug-resembling slip-ons. (The duo behind IHateCrocs.com are among us.) As attractive as a gawky, pimply teenager at the apex of his awkwardness, Crocs have enjoyed inscrutable global popularity for years now. Jack Nicholson and Halle Berry wear the things. And little Violet Affleck. President Bush sported them recently — in public — with black socks and shorts. Sigh.

Lore has it that waterproof, non-skid Crocs were

invented as a boating shoe in Boulder, Colo., by three fishing buddies. More likely: The guys were stoned and zonked out on repeats of *What Not to Wear* when one nudged the others and said: "Dude, you know what would be freaking awesome? We invent the most heinous shoes imaginable and, like, convince people they're amazing. Then see who buys 'em ..."

You really can't underestimate Americans' apathy for aesthetics, especially when comfort is a factor. By all accounts, Crocs are irresistibly cozy, which is why you should never, ever try them on. And which is why they look like something a doctor might prescribe for someone with special needs. Any shoe marketed as both "unisex" and "antimicrobial" has no business being worn outside of a restaurant kitchen or surgery ward.

I grant you that fashion is fickle and styles often grow on us after seeming odd at first. But some designs are just wrong wrong wrong from their first jaunt down the runway. Buttafuoco pants pounce to mind, as do other Emperor's New Shoes like Birkenstocks, Tevas, and even, yes, Ugg boots. (Ugg, people! Would you have bought them if they were called Yuck? Or Eww?!)

I'm not buying the "they're so ugly they're cute" logic, either. It wasn't true of the Olsen twins. It isn't true of Chihuahuas. And it doesn't make you look any less ridiculous in your lime-colored Disney Beach Crocs — especially if you're a man, in which case you ought to be ashamed of yourself.

With summer approaching, I fear frivolous-footed folk will once again be digging these eyeball-offending accessories from the back of their closets and clomping around Santa Barbara's plazas, parks, and paseos in them. But there's hope that Crocs may soon be going the way of the Pet Rock, the Clapper, the Flowbee, and other inventions that briefly convinced the nation we needed something that we really, really didn't.

The company, which only two years ago boasted the largest footwear IPO in history, recently closed its Quebec factory due to a drop in sales. And no hail-mary Mary Jane or squishy flip-flop model is going to save the brand from this freaky phenomenon: Countless Crocs-wearers, mostly children, have had their feet caught and chewed up in escalators around the globe. Last week, citing dozens of injury complaints from its most fashion-inept citizens, Japan's trade ministry called upon the manufacturer to come up with a safer design.

Ouch. Wouldn't want to be in their shoes.

Facebook Friendships Hard to Ignore

IF I WERE SHOPPING for friends, I wouldn't choose someone like me. I don't have a killer mojito recipe, a vacation home in Maui, or a cache of uproarious travel stories to share over dinner. I'm bad with birthdays. I don't even play tennis.

But suddenly everyone wants to be my pal.

I recently created an account on Facebook, the social networking site for folks too old for MySpace and too lazy for LinkedIn. No sooner had I filled out a profile than I started getting "friend requests" from people I know. And people I barely know. And people I don't know and don't want to know.

"Joe Random has added you as a friend," the alert reads. You click one button to "confirm" the friendship, another to "ignore."

I find myself wishing there was another button: "Explain." Perhaps I'm stuck on semantics, but the use of the word "friend" to describe these tenuous, meaningless digi-relationships has me confused. Who are these Facebook amigo-seekers and what exactly do they want from me?

The site itself claims: "Your friends on Facebook are the same friends, acquaintances, and family members that you communicate with in the real world."

Only they're not. Some of the "friends" I wound up with are a housewife from Long Island, a guy who never spoke to me in high school, and a complete stranger with a fondness for Lionel Richie.

My savviest Facebook friends — real friends, people I actually like — say the system is great for catching up with long-lost acquaintances. "It helps me keep tabs on what my friends are up to who I'm not likely to talk to more than once a year," said a buddy with more than 500 "friends" in his collection.

How exactly do these online alliances differ from in-person ones? "Real-life friendships grow organically," said a gal pal of mine. "Facebook friendships are superficial, instant, and often undesired."

Whereas being courted as a real-life friend is flattering, being bombarded by would-be Internet cronies is vaguely threatening. You can't tell if the request is a genuine way of saying "I like you," an attempt to look popular, or an effort to sell you something.

"I worry about the repercussions of ignoring a friend request," said my girlfriend who, like me, has more Facebook friends than she wants. "It feels weirdly hostile to say no to someone wanting to be your friend."

Everyone, it seems, has unique criteria for defining a

"friend." "Any Facebook friend of mine has to pass the wedding-announcement test," said a guy I know. "Would I tell that person if I was getting married?"

"I approve anyone who shares a number of friends with me," said another fellow. "No friends in common, no way."

A friend of mine who uses Facebook to market her product said, "A Facebook friend is someone whose money I wouldn't mind taking." Her only rule is "they can't have creepy or pornographic images on their pages."

It's easy to be cynical about the notion of making and breaking human attachments with the click of a mouse: Where do factors like trust, affection, and loyalty fit into this binary puzzle?

Still, I think this new friend-logging system has something sincere at its core: a desire for fellowship. In the isolated glow of our laptop screens, we crave a visual tally of our flesh-and-blood connections, a pixelized reminder that we have (or at least once had) contact with walking, talking, Lionel Richie-loving beings.

Ultimately, there may be no connection between Facebook friendships and real ones. No platform interface, to muddle the medium's jargon. And maybe the key to enjoying such cybercomraderie is to accept — and even celebrate — that distinction.

On a whim yesterday, I sent a friend request to comedian Bill Maher. Much to my shock, he confirmed me as a confidant — along with 1,663 other people. I'm not surprised he's got so many chums. I've heard the guy makes a killer mojito.

The Slutty Mechanic

AND OTHER FRIGHTENING HALLOWEEN COSTUMES

FORGET THE TOMBSTONES on your neighbor's lawn and the severed hand poking out of the candy bowl. The most frightening thing you'll encounter this Halloween is a middle-schooler dressed like Prudence the Naughty Pilgrim.

Any gal who's shopped for Halloween costumes during the last few years knows the get-ups are getting shorter. And tighter. And ... um ... weirder.

Slutty nun. Slutty Sherlock Holmes. Slutty Starbucks barista.

A great lover of costumes, I once hailed October 31 as a chance to inhabit other eras and vocations — as a princess or queen, cowgirl or Indian, flapper or hippy or rock star. But thanks to current costume makers, All Hallow's Eve has mutated into something very different. Something spookier, really.

A hussy's holiday. A festival of fanny flaunting.

A recent sashay through downtown's World of Magic

led me to an entire wall of itty-bitty costumes by lingerie-company-turned-costume-maker Leg Avenue. "We call it Whore Avenue," one salesgirl joked.

Gone is the once-popular sock-hop girl with shin-length poodle skirt. In her place marches the Slutty Soldier with camo mini, vinyl boots, and choker. Dead are the stately Spanish señorita and the Statue of Liberty; instead, long live the Slutty Viking, tiny-toga-sporting "Caesar's Girl" and a scantily clad Marie Antoinette — that notorious tart — in thigh-high stockings.

Guess what comes up first when you click on "Classic Women's Costumes" at BuyCostumes.com? A witch? Snow White? No. It's the Mile High Captain, a floozy airline pilot in a see-through sheath that you order by cup size.

Some costumes are classically sexy. I get that. French maid, nurse, cheerleader. Even Girl Scout, if you like that sort of thing. And I think it's fantastic if couples want to outfit themselves imaginatively for the boudoir: The Slutty Construction Worker dismounts from her front-end loader and titillating hi-jinx ensue. Hey, live it up. A gal's got to have some fun.

But when did Halloween become less about disguising your persona, and more about displaying your pumpkins? This is especially problematic for those of us with kids. Nostalgic for a Raggedy Ann costume I wore as a kid, I caved and bought a Slutty Rag Doll outfit this year — and I am trying to figure out how not to bend over while leading my little goblins through Boo at the Zoo.

If you don't want to show off your tricks or your treats, you have two basic choices in today's costume market:

Inanimate objects (spoon, bacon, Whoopee Cushion) or Stretchy the Clown, which comes in one un-sexy size: flipping ginormous.

God love the hard-bodied twentysomethings who, for a fleeting moment, have rock-solid thighs and want to parade around in as little as possible. Do it while you can, girls! But the costumes are being made for juniors, too — starting at size 0 — and that's creepy. Would you want your tween tramped out as a "Jailbird," "Fallen Angel," or "Corset Maid," a mini-dress with a "wet leather look" and "fingerless vinyl glovettes"?

Just beneath the lacy, feathered brocade of America's favorite dress-up day lays a commentary about our nation's fantasies. And I do think they're getting ickier.

Not surprisingly, there's tons of gun-toting garb: Slutty Corrections Officer, Slutty Border Patrol ("Ooh, deport me, baby ...") and Slutty FBI Agent with no pants whatsoever. There's Slutty Robin Hood (huh?) and Slutty Scarecrow (what the ...?) and even Slutty Freddy Krueger from *A Nightmare on Elm Street*. ("Okay," said my husband, who found most of the others charming. "That's just messed up.")

But wait. It gets weirder.

"They have slut dog costumes now," swears Sonia Hayward, owner of Victorian Vogue and The Costume Shoppe. "There's a naughty schoolgirl one. And wait 'til you see the Slutty Alice in Wonderland ..."

CULTURE PEARLS

Thank You For Coming

NOW GET OUT

Douse the Yule log, shelve the champagne flutes and schlep that dried-out pine tree to the curb. The party's over.

And now that Shindig Season has passed, let's resolve to be better party guests this year by learning when to set down our snifters and say, "So long." Too many promising soirées run aground when guests — caught up in the evening's convivial climate — continue to gab and gargle long after their host has started the dishwasher, thanked them for coming and opened the front door with optimism.

It's a shame, really, because you can be the most diverting guest ever to plop your rump in a patio chair. You can recount details of the time you shared a smoky limo with Mick and Keith. You can produce after-dinner truffles magically from behind your left ear.

But overstay your welcome by, say, 12 minutes and you've turned "Wow, we should have him over more often" into "Good god, don't ever let him in again." Now you're Boring Cling-On Guy.

Since party invitations rarely come with end times, it's important to learn the subtle and not-so-subtle signals that it's time to bid the bash adieu. If you're listening for them, you'll hear them.

"It's easy to be distracted if you're having a great conversation," said Melissa Lee, co-owner of Events of Santa Barbara. "But you've got to know when to say 'when.'"

At a huge event, stragglers take the hint when the catering staff begins breaking down tables and packing up decor, according to the party planner. Exit points are harder to gauge at smaller fétes, where it's the hosts' job to set the pace.

"If they're opening up another bottle of wine or engaging you in another activity — playing a game or showing you another part of the house — it's okay to stay," she said. But when they start taking off their shoes, the evening's over. And unequivocally, Lee added, "It's time to leave when someone has wet their pants."

I should point out that she has three young children, although certainly the same goes for adults.

One of my friends is exceedingly clever at chasing off clingy house guests. First she dials down her speech to monosyllabic responses. Then she leaves the room for several minutes at a time. When that fails, she asks if they need directions to the freeway — which you can literally see from her front yard.

Be creative. Conjure up a loud, open-mouth yawn, the kind that makes your face and voice contort grotesquely. Or mention the odd patch of toadstools growing in your front yard and offer to show your guests on their way out.

I also like to slip a scapegoat into the conversation, real smooth-like: "So work's keeping me busy. In fact, I've got a deadline first thing in the morning. Damn editors. They really know how to bring a dinner party to a crashing halt, am I right? But do take the rest of that cookie home with you."

I know a man who stood up from a dragging dinner party he and his wife were throwing, changed into his pajamas, flipped off every light in the house, opened the front door and said, "I'm going to bed, but don't feel like you have to leave."

While I could never be so frank, I would like to make a promise to friends who might be reading this. The next time you're at my home, and I'm ready for our socializing to come to its natural conclusion, I won't play any childish games with you. I'll simply tell you what a treat it is for my family to get to spend so much time with you.

And then I'll wet my pants.

Mancations

SOME GUYS CELEBRATE Father's Day by spending time with their families. A day at the pool. A romp on the beach.

My husband has a different request this year: to get as far away from his wife and kids as is physically, and financially, possible.

It's nothing personal, he explained, but the part of him that doesn't relish plunging toilets and wiping noses is yelping for some "me" time. Some down time.

Some man time.

So he's meeting his brother, an overworked father of three, for a weekend of childless, wifeless, workless bliss to pay tribute to Life Before Mortgage.

Before they were cast as upstanding role models for the small drink-spilling, jacket-losing, tantrum-throwing people who claim to be their children. Before they were asked to be reliable, communicative and socially demonstrative partners to calendar-keeping wives. Before they plodded happily but perhaps a bit blindly into lives as modern men who are expected to not only provide a roof over their families' heads, but mop the floors on occasion, as well.

And I get that. I do. What I don't understand is the way they choose to honor that freedom: in my spouse's case, by racing off-road all-terrain vehicles for hours on end, followed by vast over-consumption of red meat, red wine and late-night diner pie.

"I guess I want to figure out who I am besides a husband and father," he explained. "And the way it seems natural to do that is to find my limits — whether physical or gastrointestinal."

He's not alone. Guy getaways are a hot travel trend, inspiring hotels across the globe to offer testosterone-fueled packages from helicopter skiing to NASCAR training to poker parties complete with hand-rolled cigars and buckets o' beer.

There's even a moronic new term for them: "mancations." (Why not a snappy double entendre like "mandate"?) The concept, though, is nothing new. From the crowd-pleasing *City Slickers* to the Oscar-winning *Sideways* to the universally panned *Wild Hogs*, male-bonding trips have a storied history both on and off screen.

When the nagging "why, oh why" of domestic life comes into question, a furlough with the fellas can be, um, the manswer.

A friend of mine who is prone to surfing safaris, Vegas jaunts and fishing trips calls his excursions "man camp." They involve some form of friendly competition and, preferably, a modicum of danger.

"Deep conversation," he explains, "is appropriate on a case-by-case basis. For example, if I spend a week with a buddy and all I find out is that he got a new tool kit for Christmas, that is just as acceptable as learning something terribly profound. Remember, many of us communicate silently."

That is especially true, of course, if they are passed out from too much tequila. (Did you know there's an actual instrument called a "manometer" which measures — I kid you not — the pressure of gases or liquids?)

I asked my friend why he couldn't take his family along on these adventures.

"We want our wives and children to retain whatever level of esteem, admiration and affection they have for us," he says, adding ominously: "We are baser than you think."

Another friend and father of two said it would be the foul language and raunchy name-calling he would miss most if his wife and kids showed up on a husbands-only holiday.

"It would be like hosting a party during high school with your parents there," he says. "You just couldn't bust loose."

Wait, now. Cursing? Gambling? Drinking? And the pursuit of high-cholesterol, high-speed thrills with no voice of (feminine) reason in earshot?

These "mancations" aren't innocent getaways at all.

They're manarchy.

Road Trip, a.k.a Chaos in a Box

THE FLOOR IS LITTERED with apple cores, road maps, and someone's discarded socks. The smell of cattle overtakes me from time to time. And after the third hour, my butt begins to ache.

But I like it.

Road trips aren't supposed to be relished. They're the means to an end, the drag we endure so we can get to the fun part. Like a transatlantic flight beside a whiny toddler. Or an elevator ride with a stranger who's humming to himself and has Cheetos dust on his shirt.

We have no choice but to turn down our anticipation to "idle" until the motion ... comes to a full ... and complete ... stop.

Yet there's something about the magnified here-and-now of family transit — the way it forces a collective stillness — that appeals to my frazzled inner overachiever. I was reminded of this precious and peculiar pleasure during a recent road trip with my brood.

Shoehorned into my four-seater like pieces of a jigsaw puzzle, the four of us shared legroom with suitcases, portable electronics, a cooler of snacks, a diaper bag, too many jackets, and an arthritic dog dozing on a stack of CD cases. Despite our shared domicile back home, we are never all so near for so long. If one of us isn't dashing out to fetch groceries or disappearing into the garage to do laundry, the other is on the way to a basketball game or stealing a moment to check email before bed.

But not here in our car. Strapped into our 6x6-foot box, careening past farms and foothills, we have absolutely nothing to do. We can't "prepare." We can't "accomplish." We can't even catch up on reading or we'll throw up.

Forced into this state of inoccupation, we take note of things we would normally ignore. Like the filthy pickup truck beside us. "Look at the mud on that thing!" "He must have been off-roading." "Hey, why don't we ever go off-roading ... besides the filth factor, I mean?"

We make music together: me wailing, my husband rumbling bass lines, our 8-year-old playing animal-style drums on the seat back, the baby clapping spastically. We take note of the distressing number of bugs that have met their demise on our windshield and, feeling helpless in the face of such bloodshed, busy ourselves with trying to count their carcasses.

On the road, our commitment to a healthy diet is chucked out the window like the pickle from my son's fast-food cheeseburger. We allow ourselves detours for root beer floats at a roadside A&W, and brake for pancake houses that serve fluffy biscuits and gravy. We stop at a gas station and peruse the minimart's jerkies, CornNuts, and packaged pastries with a traveler's curiosity — not like they're the devil's work, but merely the regional delicacies of this strange and exotic land called Gilroy.

We take a few minutes to scamper on a pristine strip of grass at the edge of the gas station before moseying back to the car, holding hands. And I'm surprised to realize it's this aspect of road trips — the physical connection — that I like best.

In our jam-packed, litter-strewn, bug-splattered people mover, I can reach over and touch my family. Almost absentmindedly, I take one hand off the wheel to stroke my husband's cheek. I reach back and hold onto my son's calf as I drive, or squeeze the baby's feet just to reassure myself he's there.

At home, life moves faster than that maniac who just zoomed past us on the Kawasaki. But here in the car, it's suspended.

Like any good driver, I'm always scanning the road up ahead, anticipating what might be coming. I know there will be days when I miss this closeness, this instant access to my guys. And I'll cherish the hours I traded productivity for proximity.

Powerless Steering

I STILL DON'T UNDERSTAND quite how it happened. He was standing on the curb, carefully waiting to cross until the avenue was unmistakably empty.

I was watching from my car, since I had never let him cross this street by himself. This narrow but busy street.

But today he wanted to do it himself. He scoffed at my knee-jerk protests, my smothering mothering, assuring me with his eyebrows and exasperated grin that, jeez, he was almost 9, he'd done this with me a thousand times before and he could certainly navigate a straight, brightly lit, 20-foot crosswalk on his own. (The kid can say a lot with his eyebrows, trust me.)

But then there it was. Before I even knew what was happening. The careless bounding from the curb, the squeal of skidding tires and my son's fear-frozen body silhouetted against the grill of the white pickup truck that was suddenly upon him.

Every cubic millimeter of air in my lungs rushed out of

my throat in a guttural scream, and when I realized that wasn't going to be enough to stop this horror movie, I covered my eyes with my hands — which, looking back, seems like a self-indulgent thing to do.

When I uncovered them, I saw my son standing upright and ashen-faced amidst a cloud of white smoke. The truck had fishtailed sideways. The smell of burnt rubber was strong.

He bolted back to my car, leaped inside, and we both sat staring in terror out the windshield until one of us could speak.

"I don't know what to feel," he said, and burst into tears.

I knew exactly what to feel. Powerless. I have never felt so utterly useless in my whole life. If a boy's own mother can't keep him alive, for chrissake, who can?

We didn't get to meet the truck's driver before he drove away. I wanted to thank him — hell, to kiss him — for not being on his cell phone, or being drunk, or even fiddling with his radio when my son darted in front of him. (And if you're reading this, sir, please know that you will always be the example our family uses to define the word "hero.")

So we just sat together, hugging, sniffling, jittery with lingering adrenaline and trying to convince ourselves it hadn't been as ugly as it seemed. Surely the truck hadn't been as close as we thought. And look, we're both sitting here now. We're both fine. Everything's really very fine.

But in truth, we both knew how close we had come to life-snuffing tragedy. It was about five feet.

That evening, as I bid my son goodnight, he asked me

to leave his bedroom door ajar. It's a frequent request; he likes the comforting, sleep-inducing clickety-clack of my keyboard as I work at my computer downstairs. But tonight he mumbled something I didn't expect.

"Mom?" I heard him say. "Are you gonna protect me?"

And I went cold. Because clearly, as I'd demonstrated today, the answer was no. No, my precious treasure of a boy. No, I guess I'm not. I guess I can't.

"What?" I asked, looking for a clue on how to answer, how much assurance he needed in order to sleep serenely and not re-live the moment over and over in his dreams the way I knew I would tonight. And tomorrow night.

But when he repeated himself, I realized I had misheard him.

"Are you gonna be typing?" he said again, with an easy yawn.

The question hadn't been an accusation, but an affirmation. Proof that while I may not always be able to keep him safe, when life sends trauma skidding and screeching to his feet, I can at least bring him some peace.

And maybe that's the best a parent can do.

The Nana-Fest Manifesto

A LETTER TO GRANDPARENTS EVERYWHERE

WE KNOW YOU'RE BUSY right now preparing your house for our children's holiday visit. You're stocking the pantry with pancake mix and Hershey's syrup, loading the DVD player with animated "message" movies and exhuming the crayons, marbles and silly straws from the closet.

Which is great. Really. We're delighted that you adore our children, that they consider you god-like and — let's be honest — that we get free babysitting out of the deal.

But then ... nothing's really free, is it?

We wonder if you know just how truly intolerable our children are when they return to us from a week of unbridled bed-jumping and uproarious mess-making at Nana's Oreo Emporium — how lazy they become and utterly affronted they feel when asked to empty the dishwasher. Or, say, bathe.

We're guessing you don't care that we have to put our kids through Grandparent Detox since, as parents, you had to put us through the same unpleasant paces after we visited our grandparents' house. (Man, you were mean, too, and frankly we can't believe the same people who wouldn't allow a loaf of white bread into our childhood home now serve our kids Cinnabons for breakfast.)

On some level, we understand your indulgence. You've been waiting your whole lives to say "yes" to some adorable, little, wide-eyed progeny — and now that you don't have to face the long-term consequences of your own shoddy influence — have you absolutely no memory of dental bills? — you get to be the devil-may-care relatives, the fun ones.

But if you'd be kind enough to follow just these few guidelines, we promise to keep bringing your grandchildren to worship at your altar of processed sugar, poor personal hygiene and "flexible" (i.e. nonexistent) bedtimes:

1. Shockingly, our kids do know how to peel their own bananas and even pick up their socks from the floor. Sometimes, admittedly, they need reminding. Remind them.

2. Believe us when we say the children's love for you is not directly proportional to the amount of whipped cream you mound on top of their hot cocoa.

3. If you absolutely must serve root beer with lunch and grape soda with dinner, could you at least inform our children that the simple act of not serving these things does not constitute child abuse? This will help us avoid any further episodes back home in which Child Protective Services shows up at our door following up on an "amomynous" tip.

4. Demand respect. You are a wise elder of our family

tribe, so when our children talk back to you, roll their eyes or huff "whatever," lay into them, you wimpy geezer!

5. Buy them all the toys you want. But be warned that any loud electronic toys they bring home will be "accidentally" left out in the rain within two weeks of arrival. And any simulated assault weapons will be used as the centerpiece for a dinner-table lecture on man's inhumanity to man. You really don't want that on your shoulders.

6. There is nothing wrong with boredom. Boredom fosters creativity. Do you know what four solid days of ice-skating rinks and Monopoly games and Build-A-Bear workshops foster? They foster a fricking nightmare for us back home. Let the kids stare at a wall for a few minutes, will ya?

7. Please issue at least one "no" per day just to keep them familiar with the term. We understand this may be difficult for you, as the word (which, again, seemed to be your favorite utterance while we were growing up) does not come naturally to your lips these days. A simple, "No, you may not watch 'Dirty Sexy Money' with Grandpa" will do.

Signature of
Grandmother

Signature of
Grandfather

Where Are the Homeless When You Need 'Em?

WE WEREN'T TRYING to save the world. Let's face it: A hot beverage and warm brownies are token gestures, incapable of righting economic inequities or even staving off cold and hunger for more than an hour.

We only wanted one of those "shiny moments" that Oprah talks about, when you get to feel good for a second just by making someone else feel good.

Is that so wrong?

It's a family ritual of ours. We bake treats, fill travel mugs with hot cider and pile into the car to tour the town's most dazzling holiday light displays. Last year, while stopped for gas, we noticed a homeless man. It was biting cold that night. And as we sat in our steamy sedan with the heater blasting and the radio blaring "Jingle Bell Rock," we felt sick to our stomachs — and not just from the syrupy cider and peppermint brownies congealing in our guts.

Here we were headed out to celebrate the frivolity of the season, the shallow glee of ooh-ing over twinkle-lit porches and inflatable snowmen grinning from immaculate lawns. And here was this guy hugging himself on a sidewalk to keep the shivers from setting in. We couldn't help feeling we were missing the point.

We poured the fella some cider, forked over our brownies and bid him a warm and comfortable Christmas — which may well have been pointless. But it felt good.

This year, we decided to do it again, only the guy wasn't at the gas station. We drove around looking for someone who could use a hot drink, a warm gesture and a plate of gooey holiday cheer. But we couldn't find anyone. Not at the train station, on the freeway offramps, in De la Guerra Plaza. We reluctantly asked parking lot attendants: "Um, where are all the homeless people?"

Frustrated at our inability to do a good deed, we began arguing. And I'm not proud of the way our bickering illustrated a deep disconnection with life beyond our cozy middle-class existence.

Losing patience, we broadened our recipient criteria. Did the person have to actually be homeless, or was it enough to just look poor? Or sad? Or, you know, unstylish?

"There's one! I'm pulling over." "No, that guy's listening to an iPod!" "Well ... everyone has an iPod these days, that doesn't mean he isn't hungry." "Come on, Dad, just give it to him, the cider's getting cold."

"There! That lady's just sitting on that bench." "That's a bus stop, honey. She's waiting for a bus." "Well, that can't be pleasant ..."

We were about to give up when we spotted him walking up State Street. A man in a hat and thin jacket, carrying a giant bag of ... something. Was it recyclables plucked from trash cans?

"Excuse me, sir?" my husband hollered out the window. "Would you like some hot cider and brownies?"

He approached our car and the quizzical look on his face convinced us we'd made a terrible mistake and that he was about to tell us, as nicely as possible, that he wasn't homeless and that his bag was filled with Christmas presents he had just purchased from Saks Fifth Avenue on an Amex Platinum card.

But no.

"The only problem," he said, "is that I don't have a cup."

"You do now," I said, handing him a travel mug.

"Oh, wow!" he said. "Really? Thanks a lot!"

It didn't change the world. We can't even claim to have learned much from the experience. But I'll say this: As far as shiny moments go, I'll take the gleam of a stranger's smile over a glowing lawn reindeer any day.

Ode to Real Love

IT WAS FOREVER AGO, I know. But not so long ago that I've forgotten. The feelings trickle back through me when I hear Jane's Addiction or catch a glimpse of your thrift-store wingtips at the back of the closet. If I close my eyes and remember, the sensations flood right back to the surface:

That fluttery-gut feeling of our earliest days together. The intoxicating cocktail of elation, lust, and panic. The sheer shock of being adored. And the profligate peace of staying in bed 'til 2 p.m., then venturing out for a sloppy three-dollar breakfast, inhaled while holding hands.

We used to do everything holding hands. Drive. Sleep. Shower. As if we were afraid these extraordinary feelings would slip away if we let go to scratch an itch ...

We don't hold hands much anymore. Though we share a home now (and hallelujah, a still-sizzlin' boudoir), casual contact is harder to come by. A peck on the cheek as we rush out the door, a quick shoulder rub standing at the stove, a semi-conscious pre-dawn spoon. I can't remember the last time we stayed in bed past 8 a.m., fingers entwined.

Of course I miss it. I miss the dopey glee and oddly pleasant ache of dewy new romance. I'll bet you do, too.

But we had those things already. We celebrated those Valentine's Days and — ahem, if memory serves — we celebrated them good. So today let's toast the rest of this relationship. The part we didn't see cooking: the considerable cupcake of marriage beneath the flashy frosting of courtship.

The fact is, I don't swoon for guys in bands, or motorcycle jackets, anymore. Which is perfect because you're not one and don't wear them anymore. Blame maturity, that old killjoy, but it isn't rebellion, showmanship, or the tortured soul of an artist that turns me on now. It's compassion, courage, and capability. And baby, you got 'em.

I get a gut-twisting crush on you every time you fix something: Internet router. Rearview mirror. Clogged toilet. I don't know how to do those things. I've tried, and I can't. If you weren't around, I would literally have to call a plumber or flirt with our neighbor just to get someone to plunge the loo. Thank you for not making me do that.

I cherish the way you make a point of saying, "Hi, beautiful" when I'm sick with the flu and have tissues stuffed up my nose because I got tired of blowing it. And the way you grit your teeth and let me put my utterly bloodless feet up against your warm legs when I skitter into bed at night. Sometimes you whimper, or explain,

"You know how good that feels to you? That's how bad it feels to me." But you never push me away.

Never. Not when I'm crabby. Or whiny. Or weepy. Not even when you really should.

I adore that you don't like dancing, but you love dancing with me. And that you're always the funniest guy in the room, and nobody but me knows it. And that you don't notice my wrinkles, or at least say you don't notice, which is the exact same thing as far as I'm concerned.

Young love may promise the thrill of the unknown: What perfume will he like best? What makes her angry? But one part I don't miss is the anxiety over "what's next?" Hoping we'll keep enjoying each other. Wondering if we'll last.

We did. This is what it looks like. It's different than how we started out. Faster. Fuller. And granted, sometimes a little flatter. But with my newfound maturity and your proven competence, I'll bet we can rustle up some time to hold hands today.

Meet me in the shower.

My Father's Gift

IT'S BEEN TWO YEARS since we discovered my father was having an affair.

For the last 12 years, the moral center of our family had been outwardly manning the grill at backyard barbecues, treating my mother to coffee in bed every morning, whisking his grandson off to the zoo. But secretly, he'd been sending another woman roses. Telling her he loved her. Giving her nicknames none of us had ever heard, and making himself at home in a house — in a neighborhood — none of us even knew existed.

The fallout was hideous, as you might imagine. Screaming. Pleading. Nausea. Sleeplessness. Broken pottery. And enough tears to fill the swimming pool where we had always spent summers floating peacefully, ignorantly.

There was so much crying — four generations bawled intermittently — that we became desensitized to it and could eventually sit and watch each other sob without offering a hug, fetching a Kleenex, or trying to say something reassuring. Through blurry eyes we watched three decades of mutual reliance, respect, and devotion wash away.

My mother said the worst part is he never could tell us why he did it — and that he seemed okay with letting us wonder. Friends think the worst part was the duration of the affair; a slip of the will is forgivable, a decade of deception diabolical.

For me, the worst part was the walloping flood of disappointment that came with learning the one person I upheld as ever-giving, ever-strong, ever-true was truly selfish. Truly weak. Truly false. But there are so many "worst parts" it's hard to rank them.

My parents divorced. My father moved away and, perhaps tragically, neither he nor I have made much effort to stay in touch. There's too much bad water still sloshing around between us, lapping at our increasingly distant shores: shame on his end, resentment on mine.

Now that the wounds are starting to scab, and we can actually picture the rest of our lives without him, and we are able to utter things like, "I guess you never really know somebody the way you think you do" without our throats closing up in that familiar, tiresome way — now there's a new worst part. Learning to re-love him.

As much as I prefer the burn of anger to the sting of sorrow, as much as I rather enjoy the lingering flavor of a nice beefy grudge, it turns out you can't fully write off a parent.

There's a weird thing that happens when you've been betrayed by someone you love. First you reevaluate every fond memory that enters your head: When he wrote that beautiful poem for my wedding, did he read it to her first? When he came to meet his first grandson in the hospital, was he wishing he was somewhere else?

But eventually, fond memories begin to creep in without first being run through the Hostility Filter. Things he says that make me laugh, no matter how often he says them. His magic tricks that never fail to dazzle a crowd. The way dogs, cats, and dull people always gravitate toward him, much to his dismay.

I didn't send my dad a present for Father's Day this year; I couldn't bring myself to do it. Instead, perhaps I'll celebrate the gifts he's given me — the values he modeled so beautifully when ... well, when I knew him best.

We share a passion for peanut butter, a love of driving, a reverence for Bill Cosby. His heroes are mine, and his politics. His favorite songs are mine, and his sense of humor. If dishonesty is what carved our family's rift, then let's be honest: My father is me. And I'm him.

I guess you never really know somebody the way you think you do.

The Stuff Slough

SORTING AND SIFTING
THE SOUVENIRS OF SEVEN DECADES

IT WAS CANCER, and it all happened faster than we expected. Not 24 hours after my mother-in-law's ashes were scattered at sea, I found myself sitting on her bed, staring blankly into her bedroom closet, with a trash bin beside me.

Nancy was a generous woman who spent her whole life giving. It wasn't until we peeked into her long-shut cabinets and wrestled open her overstuffed drawers that we realized how much receiving she had done. And collecting. And clipping. And buying. And generally, alarmingly, amassing.

She just had way too much stuff. More than she could have fully enjoyed in any lifetime, even one that hadn't been cut short at age 70. And it fell to us — her grieving sons and daughters-in-law — to "go through her things," sorting and sifting the souvenirs of her seven decades.

Knitting needles and antique hats. Greeting cards and hotel soaps. Place mats and curling irons.

We trudged through as many emotions as we did half-empty bottles of nail polish: The shame of poking around in someone's private stashes. The frustration of not knowing what this key opens, or what to do with Great Aunt Catherine's geodes. The guilt from allowing practical considerations to squelch sentiment — from giving away, or throwing away, things that were surely precious to their owner, but had no special meaning to those of us on the Hefty Bag Brigade.

I wondered why the family was in such a hurry to clear her clutter. Couldn't it wait, for goodness' sake? The woman was barely gone and here we were disposing of evidence that she existed.

The work was therapeutic, though. Illness wrests control from a human being, from a family, and hard work lets us feel like we're reclaiming it. Death brings emotional chaos; resolute tidiness restores order. So in the unfathomable absence of an always-present mother, we focused on indisputable tangibles: Her lipstick. Her teacup. Her shoes.

From beneath teetering sweater piles, we exhumed cheering memories, fingering the fancy scarves she wore and sniffing the candles she set out last Thanksgiving.

But much of what we unearthed was unsettling. Every tote bag and trunk held a disheartening reminder of her unmet goals and dreams: Gifts — some of them wrapped — that never got given. Recipes that never got made. A pair of jazz shoes without a single scuff. An astonishing inventory of unopened wrinkle creams. A library of how-to books whose objectives, from simple craft projects to ambitious entrepreneurship, proved ever out of her reach.

What bothered me was not that the projects were unfinished. It was that they were never really started. I'm haunted by a series of small jewelry boxes scattered throughout the house, each cradling a tiny silver charm representing her favorite things: the Eiffel Tower, a sewing machine, a cable car … And each had a price tag still attached. Never linked to the nearly bare charm bracelet curled up in yet another buried box. Never worn.

Nancy wouldn't have loved us trodding through her tucked-away stuff. Nor, frankly, would she have wanted strangers to read about it. But she'd have been glad at what it taught me: That you can't hold life in your hands. You can't wear it, stockpile it, or cram it into cubbies for safe keeping. You can't divvy it up into boxes marked "Garbage," "Goodwill," and "Grandkids." And you can't measure it by the number of dumpsters it takes to dismantle.

Life doesn't live in the things that we have. It takes place in the things that we do: coming and going, building and bonding, laughing and even grieving.

Nancy cherished her tchotchkes, to be sure. But she'd have traded them all for another chance to scuff those dance shoes.

Merry Solstice

LOOKING BACK, I NEVER really had a shot at being pious. With a lapsed Catholic for a mother and a secular Jew for a stepfather, I was a spiritual orphan, destined to stumble through the year-end holidays with no real sense of history.

Oh, sure, we decorated a Christmas tree and lit a menorah. I could play "Silent Night" on the piano and recite the Hanukkah prayer in Hebrew — feats that made grandparents on both sides beam.

But the geneses of these religious holidays were unclear to me, and their stories a holly jolly jumble. I was convinced, for instance, that a drummer boy chased the Syrians out of Israel and holed up in a temple, where he had the chutzpah to keep Rudolph's nose aglow for all 12 days of Christmas — a miracle if I ever heard one!

Mangers and Maccabees, virgins and latkes. These symbols were as irrelevant to me as snowmen and sleigh rides in our sunny Southern California suburb. They were just myths to give colorful backstory to the indulgent rituals we couldn't otherwise justify: overeating, overspending, and running up the electric bill to make our home sparkle like the Gates of Heaven — whatever those were.

But when I grew up and began guiding my own children through the holidays, I felt a bit … I don't know … untethered. My household possesses the requisite love of nog, twinkle lights, and Douglas fir. But our family's beliefs just aren't reflected in the lyrics to "O Come All Ye Faithful" or the teachings of the Talmud.

And it occurred to me recently, that's a total rip-off. So I began poking around for something my brood could really rejoice over, something monumental and magical that would make us feel connected, inspired — even reverent.

Kwanzaa's cool, but its 1966 origin makes the African-American holiday too modern for my taste. I wanted a ritual that had been around — humming happily just under the organized-religion radar — for centuries. I found it in winter solstice.

Occurring every December 21 or 22, the solstice is the shortest day and longest night of the year. Technically the first day of winter, it's also the gateway to spring, the moment after which days begin to grow longer again. For thousands of years, pagans (non-Christians) celebrated the solstice as an annual rebirth of the sun; a promise that spring and summer were on their way; a reminder that even when life is darkest and coldest, there is light and warmth around the bend. Now there's something I can say "amen" to.

Ancient folk believed the only way to coax the sun back

into the sky was to throw it a wild, wintery party with much feasting and wine. (Are you with me here?) Turns out lots of the symbols we associate with Christmas — wreaths, holly, evergreen boughs, mistletoe, yule logs — were actually, er, borrowed from pagan solstice celebrations.

So my family borrowed 'em right back. Now every year, we light a yule log and toss leaves into the fire to cast away memories we'd like to leave behind. We sing the yuletide carol "Deck the Halls" and make silent wishes for the coming year. We light four candles representing the seasons and talk about the joys of each. Together, we chant a short poem about sunlight and then hug and open presents.

Some might think it's weird, but we don't sacrifice a goat or anything. And we haven't even given up Christmas or Hanukkah; I still love the feel of Hebrew prayers on my tongue and the warble of a heartfelt "O Holy Night." We've just added more colorful lore to the seasonal mix so that my children will have a stronger grasp of holiday history than I ever did.

Like the "fact," ahem, that Santa hails from Stonehenge.

Me Time

LONELY? I DON'T UNDERSTAND THE QUESTION

SURELY I HEARD him wrong.

"I think I'll take the boys camping over your birthday weekend," my husband had said, "and give you some time to yourself."

As a freelance writer with two young sons and eight employers at any given instant, my "me time" is confined to the shower and the car, driving to fetch someone from somewhere — not time for myself, just time by myself.

So his offer sounded absurd. I ran it through my trusty guilt check: I didn't ask, he offered. They love camping, I hate it. It is my birthday.

I'm shocked by the lump in my throat as my family drives away. Is it instinctive grief over losing control of my flock? Or (gulp) a fear that I won't know what to do with myself when they're gone?

But I'm more shocked at how quickly I get over it. No sooner have I bolted the front door than I am giddily — almost maniacally — reclaiming the house as my own. I put toys away and they stay there. I belt Bob Seger songs and no one leaves the room. I share my dinner with the dog without setting a bad example for anyone.

The words "sensible" and "balanced" have no sway over my meals for three whole days. I eat when I'm hungry, which is every 85 minutes or so. I walk to the farmers market because I'm craving a peach. I stop by the cupcake shop and inhale a ginormous chocolatey mound while standing up. I share it with no one. I sit at counters rather than wait for tables. I order champagne with lunch.

The Central Coast's offerings feel vast, even profligate, when nap times and boredom protests needn't be factored into the schedule. I spend two and a half hours at Target because I can, wandering aisles full of crap I neither need nor want, grinning like a woman on wondrous anti-depressants.

I drive slowly and without honking. I'm in no hurry. No one is waiting for me. No one is starving. And if I'm late, no one will pout.

I pop into a cheapo nail salon and wait 40 minutes for a pedicure. I don't care. I read. I listen to conversations, to accents. I inhale acetone and am happy. Or just high, but why differentiate? There is no one knocking things over, digging through my purse for candy, or grabbing their pants in a way that suggests an "accident" is imminent. (Note: My spouse rarely does this.)

I go to a movie by myself. It's not fantastic, but I laugh louder than anyone else because I don't have to explain the joke, or cringe at the language, or pay close attention so I can discuss the plot afterward. I just watch, laugh and leave. It's crazy.

And something else happens. My radar reorients. Long trained to scan the horizon for things my family needs right now (sunscreen? smoothie?) and things it's likely to need three hours from now (pep talk? pudding cup?), my sensors turn tentatively inward. I'm suddenly, startlingly aware of how I feel. Mildly tired but playful and … even contemplative. It's odd to be so in touch with myself, to respond so generously and immediately to my own quiet urges.

I keep waiting to feel lonely but it never comes, because I know my guys are coming back. When they finally burst through the front door, I feel more alive, more conscious, more cared for than when they left.

"Did you miss us?" they ask, handing me their laundry.

"Terribly," I moan, my radar reverting back to its outward orientation. But inside I'm chuckling.

Surely I heard them wrong.

Diary of a Protest Virgin

UNTIL THIS SUMMER, I had never protested anything in my life. My mother burned her bra in New York City in 1967 in support of women's rights, then marched around Manhattan braless afterward, an experience she describes, ironically, as "uplifting." But I hail from the Slacker generation, a group of jaded navel gazers so lazy that our loudest public outcry to date has been the collective "bummer" mumbled the day Starbucks discontinued its Raspberry Mocha Chip Frappuccino. (Why? Why!)

Over the last three months, though, while protesting the management policies of my former employer, the *Santa Barbara News-Press*, I learned that standing up for what you know to be right is exhilarating. It's also frightening. And when you're trying to look defiant in front of TV news cameras as your kitten heels sink into the grass of the public plaza, well, it's awkward at best.

What I never knew before I raised my first public fist

of power is that, whether you're torching undergarments or demanding integrity in the press, righteous indignation can be freaking exhausting. It's tough, you see, to sustain both the energy and decorum required of a juicy and drawn-out public fight. You must be the very model of a sober soldier, though you've never needed a drink so badly in your life. You must ever endeavor to embody the morality of your cause, despite your gnawing inclination to say something truly profane to your direct supervisor.

Twice.

Former colleagues of mine let their gardens go to seed and their bills pile up while they made phone calls to lawyers, collected signatures from subscribers, wrote press releases, distributed posters and hunted down sound equipment for our protests.

This tug between the Right to Assemble and the Need to Have Groceries threatened to tear me in two on the day of a major public rally, during which we reporters had agreed to stand in solidarity, wearing black to signify the solemnity of our professional situation:

My infant son awakes with a raging fever and drippy nose, making him unwelcome at day care. My dryer breaks, leaving me to choose between two categories of black clothing — too wet and too slutty. I arrive at the rally late. With bad hair. And snot on my shoulder.

The event's speeches — probably very inspiring — are drowned out by a continuous news scroll in my head that reads, "No food in the house. ... How much is a new dryer? ... Column due in two hours ... Can babies get bird flu?"

That evening, while dashing through Trader Joe's

with my sick son, I am interviewed via cell phone by a reporter from another paper. I'm knocking food into my cart, shoving Cheerios into the baby's frowning pie hole, and failing to sound profound or even literate when I drop a container of lemon yogurt on the floor. It splatters across my shoes, and those of everyone around me.

I am not noble David in the face of Goliath. I am Larry, Moe and Curly with a picket sign.

For me, the finest moments of the News-Press conflict so far have been recognizing the good company of the protesters around me — in the ribcage-rattling chant of rightfully angry readers, or the collective yelp and subsequent laughter of my fellow journalists as we ripped the duct tape from our mouths before heading back to work.

Now that I've experienced the unique adrenaline rush of agitation, you'll probably see me at more protests: political marches, perhaps a sit-in or two. But I'd like to go on record as saying that when it comes to standing up for one's rights, I don't think bra-burning is the way to go. Protesting, it turns out, isn't something you want to enter into without support.

If I Ran the Zoo

A TRIBUTE TO DR. SEUSS ON HIS BIRTHDAY

For a century now, it has sat in this spot.
    And the townsfolk have liked it. They've liked it a lot.
    But the Pleasantville Zoo saw some changes the day
That a fat cat decided she must have her way.

"It's a pretty good zoo," said Ms. Hootie McWho
"And the people who work there seem competent, too.
But if I ran the zoo, if I bought it from you,
I would make a few changes. That's just what I'd do.

"There are too many critters, I tell you, too many.
In the new zoo, McWho's Zoo, there will not be any.
There will be no more monkeys, no meerkats, no mice.
Because animals shouldn't be caged. It's not nice.

"I'll free all the geckos, the sloths and the skinks
And the blood-sucking poisonous toads (those poor things).
I'll release the flamingos, the crane and the pheasant,
And the screeching macaw, which I find rather pleasant.

"This new zoo will be cool! It will be so un-cruel!
It will be the town's pride! It will be the town's jewel!
Oh, but wait now, just wait. There's a problem I see:
Namely, who wants a zoo that is animal-free?

"Empty dens, empty pens, empty cages and pools ...
The town may not notice. Let's face it. They're fools.
Ah, but here's an idea. Never mind the giraffe.
Why not have some real fun? Why not lock up ... the staff?

"Yes, it's perfect! I'll lock up the staff on the double.
For when they roam free, they are nothing but trouble.
I'll corral every hard-working uniformed bloke
from the cage-mucking boy to that gal who sells Coke.

"And I tell you, those workers will make quite a show.
They will rattle their cages! Just look at them go!
I will teach them to juggle and smile and say 'Please.'
I will teach them to do it from down on their knees.

"When all three of my friends come to visit my zoo,
We can heckle my pets and flick rocks at them, too.
And just think — oh just think — how much fun it will be!
And the whole stinking planet will wish it were me! ..."

Almost nobody visits the Zoo anymore.
With no gnus to be found there, it's really a bore.
But Ms. Hootie McWho is not lonely, far from it.
She's hired new hapless zoo workers to run it.

One by one, as her beasties escape from their pens,
She just locks up the poor serfs who mucked out their dens.
Cuz no matter how far your ideas may be flung ...
You can always find someone to shovel your dung.

Taking the Stand

YES, I DO SOLEMNLY SWEAR

THE WORLD IS RIFE with judges.
Not the robed kind, necessarily, but folks who want to size us up according to surface traits that belie our greater sense of self.

Order an extra cocktail and you're labeled an alcoholic; turn it down and you're a killjoy. Confess you hate to exercise and suddenly you're a slacker; admit you love it and you're a shallow-minded, image-obsessed, endorphin-addicted freak (maybe I'm the only one who thinks that).

In our youth, we resist such labels. I recall as a teen feeling panicked at my inability to prevent strangers — teachers, dentists, really cute boys — from branding me as something I wasn't. Slut. Prude. Brain. Ditz. Dork. Rebel. In truth, I was any number of those things but didn't know it yet.

With adulthood comes the sweet relief of a thicker skin, and a healthy but hard-earned disinterest in what people think of us. But I was recently sucked into an odd bubble of self-consciousness that rivaled that of my adolescence. I was called as a witness in a federal hearing, and although I wasn't personally on trial, my credibility and character were called into question.

Which is nothing personal, of course. In a court of law, a witness is not a flawed, well-meaning human being with complicated motivations. You are simply a piece of evidence in a pinstriped jacket — no more or less dimensional than a signed document or a lock of hair in a forensics baggie. If you have something to say that will make one set of lawyers happy, it's the other lawyers' job to make you look like a devious fruitcake.

Still, knowing your integrity is about to be poked and prodded in the public record is unnerving. And as my court date approached, I became frightfully aware of every personal failing, public indiscretion, and lapse of citizenship that could possibly be tied to my name: abundant front-yard weeds, countless California stops, refusal to volunteer as Room Parent for my son's fourth-grade class … the list, I'm afraid, goes on.

What if they got testimony from all the waiters I've tipped abominably? Or photos of me at McDonald's last week feeding my toddler French fries for dinner while sitting outside, in front of god and everyone?

The truth is I'm not forthright in every aspect of my life. I color my hair, I ink over the scuff marks on my shoes with black Sharpie, and don't make me tell you about my padded bra. ("Ms. Roshell, if you're such an honest person, the court demands to know why you present yourself to all the world as a B-cup!" The courtroom gasps.) But once my miscreant keister finally found itself in the witness chair, I discovered some delightful things.

First, if you're called to court one day but never make it to the stand because things are proceeding so slowly, you can wear the exact same thing again the next day and not a single person will notice. I swear.

Second, unless you're instructed to holler expletives across the room, as I was — which, to be honest, feels a bit like wailing "Sympathy for the Devil" during a Catholic mass — courtrooms are not as scary as they seem.

Sure, you need a hearty hide (in part because courtrooms are kept at goose bump-inducing temperatures to prevent accidental napping). But it turns out you don't need much else, because a witness's job is neither to prove nor disprove anything. It's simply to tell the truth — a task that even this cheapskate, bleachy-headed slacker mom found to be surprisingly easy.

But then, who am I to judge?

How to Love Hate Mail

I'M SURE I DON'T have to tell you that my job — courageously and painstakingly cataloging the minutiae of my life — is extremely dangerous, if obviously rewarding, work. One is harangued by hecklers at every turn. Hecklers with access to a thesaurus, it seems.

But they teach me things, my detractors. Like when I think I've written something pithy and fresh, for example, they inform me it's actually "ignorant and insulting drivel." Or "revolting and self-indulgent." Or even "a constant revelation of pitiful values," which is important information for any writer to have about her work. Crucial, really.

Readers take issue with everything from my name and photo to my choice of topics and apparently flaccid sense of humor. They cast aspersions on my mothering ("How will your child turn out if this represents your view of society?"), my daughtering ("I hope your mother still speaks to you after she reads this article"), and even my granddaughtering ("You must not have loved your grandparents").

It's funny what people get riled up about. The columns I think will be most controversial are often read with a sniff and a yawn; others, intended merely as bites of amusement to be enjoyed with coffee, seem to launch passionate community-wide debates. Or at least a lot of online name-calling — which is fun, too.

I've been called a poor-mannered whiner and an insecure control freak with "an attitude of smug condensation." I believe the author meant smug condescension, but I like the error so much that it is now a favorite phrase around my house. As in "Mom, how come I can see my breath on cold mornings?" "Just ignore it, dear. It's just that smug condensation again."

Some readers are not so much offended by my words as they are concerned for my soul. I get invited to church more often than I can laugh about.

There's consolation, I suppose, in the fact that my column inspires readers toward heartfelt honesty and thoughtful metaphors, like the guy who stopped reading, then wrote to tell me, "I miss your column like I miss a root canal." If I can help just one subscriber find his creative voice, well then …

But the critiques I enjoy most are those that are poorly written (I confess to forwarding them to my smugly condensed friends), and those that are right on the money, calling me out on my crap. Here are some recent favorites:

"Which came first: the desire for a hole in your nose

or the desire to write a column about putting a hole in your nose?"

"Who is this woman, and does a third-grader do her hair?"

"So life's too short for oral hygiene, huh? You're a real catch! Here's a tip that will save you lots more time, and money, too: Stop using toilet paper! Just think of it. With all the time you've been wasting wiping your ass you could have written the Great American Novel by now!"

There's one especially caustic reader with short-term memory loss who repeatedly pelts me with insults, always ending his rant with the promise that one day my breasts will droop, and then I'll be sorry.

I'm usually quite diplomatic when responding to criticism; if I'm going to ask readers to care about my whims and fancies, I should at least be willing to hear theirs. But after one of the boob guy's tirades accused me of being a wimp and a liberal mouthpiece and questioned my ability to hold on to a man, I could remain silent no longer. I responded thusly: "With all due respect, sir, you are way off base. My breasts are nowhere near big enough to sag."

★ Index ★

Anaphylactic shock, 155
Astro Blasters, 172
Ba-donk-a-donk, 56
Belgian coeds, 61
Bicuspids, 26, 127
Colony Collapse Disorder, 105
Cruella de Vil, 78
Cupcakes, 58, 112, 142, 157, 237, 249
Duncan Hines, 158
Embalming fluid, 192
Endorphin-addicted freak, 259
Firming lotion, 57
Flush monkey, 160
Gag reflex, 105
Galapagos finches, 36
Genitals, 36, 43, 49, 111
George Clooney, 39
Goldfish cracker, 124
Goodnight, Gorilla, 29
Hefty Bag Brigade, 243
Ichthys fish, 108
Inglorious Bastards, 79
Jack Daniels, 182
Jedi Camp, 139
Jesus, 72, 94
Latex gloves, 87
Lollapalooza, 30
Lube, 17
Manarchy, 223
Nana's Oreo Emporium, 230
Narcissistic Acid-Head, 188
Nipples, 23
Odysseus, 164
Old Glory, 74
Perennially canoodling, 104
Prudence the Naughty Pilgrim, 212
Screeching macaw, 257
Smug condensation, 263
Solar-Powered Mole Repeller, 179
Sphincter, 105
Stripper poles, 17
Ted Haggard, 93
Terri Gross, 195
Venti Macchiato, 129
Violet Affleck, 206
War-mongering gladhander, 68
Willy-nilly, 92
Wonderbra, 47
Vaginoplasty, 48
Viper Room, 35
Zsa Zsa, 150

About the Author

NAMED FOR A SONG in the 1960s musical "Hair," Starshine Roshell is a freelance journalist and syndicated columnist. The winner of a California Newspaper Publisher's Association award for best column writing, She resigned from the *Santa Barbara News-Press* in 2006 in protest of management's ethics. Her columns now appear in the *Santa Barbara Independent, Ventura Star, Roanoke Times* and on *ParentClick* web sites throughout the country.

Starshine teaches journalism at Santa Barbara City College and writes for *Westways, Santa Barbara Magazine, Destination Wine Country, Miller-McCune, 805 Living* and *Hybrid Mom*. She wrote the children's books "Real-Life Royalty" and "A Day in the Life of a Fashion Designer" and was an author of the insider's guide "Hometown Santa Barbara."

Printed in the United States
130154LV00004B/112-570/P